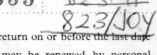

THE ART
OF
JAMES JOYCE

First draft of the opening to *Finnegans Wake*
(Courtesy of the British Museum)

THE ART
OF
JAMES JOYCE

Method and Design in *Ulysses*
and *Finnegans Wake*

BY

A. WALTON LITZ

Et ignotas animum dimittit in artes

LONDON
OXFORD UNIVERSITY PRESS
NEW YORK   TORONTO
1961

Oxford University Press, Amen House, London E.C.4

GLASGOW NEW YORK TORONTO MELBOURNE WELLINGTON
BOMBAY CALCUTTA MADRAS KARACHI KUALA LUMPUR
CAPE TOWN IBADAN NAIROBI ACCRA

Printed in Great Britain

PREFACE

WHEN I first undertook this investigation of Joyce's methods of composition, and began to examine the drafts and proof-sheets of *Ulysses* and *Finnegans Wake*, I was confident that these sources would ultimately provide me with a thread for the labyrinth. Like most critics of Joyce, I had been lured by the multiple designs of his art into believing that somewhere there existed one controlling design which contained and clarified all the others. For a time it seemed as if this might be true. Joyce's incessant revisions present a clear record of his evolving artistic aims, as well as incidental clues to the meaning of specific passages; and in the case of *Finnegans Wake* the early drafts are often the best running commentary on the finished work. But somehow the controlling design that I sought eluded me, and I have long since relinquished the comforting belief that access to an author's workshop provides insights of greater authority than those produced by other kinds of criticism. The irreducible gap between the creator and his work faces one at every turn. Indeed it now seems to me that the controlling design—the 'figure in the carpet'—lies always in plain view, not in the dark corners explored by the genetic or biographical critic. Therefore I claim no special authority for this study, although I have tried to found my conclusions on a factual survey of the manner in which *Ulysses* and *Finnegans Wake* achieved their final forms.

The obvious limitations of the present study were inherent in my purpose. It was my intention to write a 'biography' of *Ulysses* and *Finnegans Wake*, tracing the growth of each work and using this evidence to document Joyce's shifting artistic ideals. My main interest was in technique, and I sought to discover how the methods of the *Wake* developed out of those of *Ulysses*. During the seven years he spent in writing *Ulysses* and the sixteen years devoted to *Finnegans Wake* Joyce's techniques underwent radical changes, yet when the various stages of composition are examined we receive an impression of gradual evolution in method and design which is not conveyed by the finished works. This study should supply further proof of the essential unity in Joyce's achievement.

I have focused my attention on *Ulysses* and *Finnegans Wake* for several reasons. Joyce's poetry and his one play, *Exiles*, are not considered because they stand outside the main stream of his technical development and present special problems peculiar to their *genres*. The exclusion of *Dubliners, Stephen Hero* and *Portrait of the Artist* may seem less defensible, but in all these early works Joyce was accommodating his art to techniques that were already characteristic of advanced English and French fiction. His unique contribution to modern literature is found mainly in his last two works, where new techniques are introduced in an effort to express areas of consciousness previously unexplored. Furthermore, information on Joyce's earlier works is readily available, and anyone who wishes to assess his stylistic development between 1904 and 1914 can do so by comparing *Stephen Hero* with *A Portrait of the Artist as a Young Man*.

Although I have aimed at a fusion of critical and scholarly methods, hoping that they will support each other, some chapters are necessarily quite factual. The opening chapters of Parts I and III, which trace the evolution of *Ulysses* and the *Wake*, are primarily concerned with the details of composition, and their chronological structure may strike some readers as excessively detailed; but without the evidence provided by these chapters the conclusions put forward elsewhere would have little validity. I hope that the book will be read as a unit since it was written with a single intention, to record and assess Joyce's artistic development between 1914 and 1939. If any further justification for my strategy is needed I can only plead, with Dr. Johnson, that 'it is pleasant to see great works in their seminal state' and 'to trace their gradual growth and expansion'.

This examination of Joyce's mature techniques is somewhat specialized, and for that I am sorry. It was written for the reader who knows Joyce's work and some of the major critical positions, but I have tried to avoid unnecessary reliance on the minutiae of a critical literature which has reached appalling proportions. In recent years the need for general surveys of Joyce's art (such as those of Stuart Gilbert, Harry Levin and W. Y. Tindall) has been filled, and Joycean criticism has entered a phase of consolidation distinguished by a number of specific studies. My work belongs to this phase, and like most special studies it is dependent on the accomplishments of earlier scholars and critics.

In a somewhat different form this book was a dissertation submitted for the degree of Doctor of Philosophy in Oxford University. For assistance in preparing that early version I am indebted to H. V. D. Dyson, of Merton College, Oxford, and M. J. C. Hodgart, of Pembroke College, Cambridge. I am also greatly indebted to the following for information and encouragement: John Bryson, Balliol College, Oxford; Frank Budgen; Thomas Connolly, University of Buffalo; Richard Ellmann, Northwestern University; Fred Higginson, Kansas State College; Marvin Magalaner, City College of New York; Joseph Prescott, Wayne State University; Lawrance Thompson, Princeton University; the staff of the British Museum, especially George Painter and Julian Brown; the Cornell University Library; the Lockwood Memorial Library, University of Buffalo, especially Miss Anna Russell; the Princeton University Library; the Philip and A. S. W. Rosenbach Foundation, Philadelphia; and the Yale University Library. Parts of this book originally appeared in PMLA, *Modern Fiction Studies*, *Philological Quarterly*, and *A James Joyce Miscellany: Second Series*. I am indebted to the James Joyce Estate and the Society of Authors for permission to quote passages from the Joyce manuscripts. I am deeply grateful to the

Research Council of Princeton University for grants which supported much of my basic research and aided in the publication of this study.

For permission to quote from the works of James Joyce I am indebted to the Society of Authors, literary representatives of the Joyce Estate, and to the following publishers: in the United States, The Viking Press (quotations from *Finnegans Wake*, *Portrait of the Artist*, *Exiles*, ed. Padraic Colum, *The Letters of James Joyce*, ed. Stuart Gilbert) and Random House (quotations from *Ulysses*); in England, Faber & Faber (quotations from *Finnegans Wake*), The Bodley Head (quotations from *Ulysses*), and Jonathan Cape (*Portrait of the Artist*). I must also thank Frank Budgen, David Daiches, and Charles Scribner's Sons (publishers of *Axel's Castle* by Edmund Wilson) for permission to quote material.

To Harriet Shaw Weaver, who generously allowed me to examine much of the unpublished material then in her possession, and who patiently gave her attention to the many questions she alone could answer from personal experience, I owe the greatest debt of all. Her unceasing interest in the progress of Joyce's reputation is an inspiration to all who would study his work. Without her assistance this book could never have been written in its present form.

ABBREVIATIONS

PAGE references for *Ulysses* and *Finnegans Wake* are inserted directly in the text, preceded by 'U' or 'FW'. I have used the Modern Library (Random House) text of *Ulysses*, and all quotations have been checked against the authoritative Odyssey Press edition (Third Impression, Hamburg, 1935). A table for converting the pagination of the Random House *Ulysses* into that of the English edition (John Lane, The Bodley Head) is provided at the end of the notes for Section I. In referring to *Finnegans Wake* I have often given both page and line numbers, separating the two by a stroke. The English and American editions of the *Wake* have the same pagination.

In referring to the episodes of *Ulysses* I have used the Homeric titles which Joyce assigned them.

1. *Telemachus*	10. *Wandering Rocks*
2. *Nestor*	11. *Sirens*
3. *Proteus*	12. *Cyclops*
4. *Calypso*	13. *Nausicaa*
5. *Lotus-eaters*	14. *Oxen of the Sun*
6. *Hades*	15. *Circe*
7. *Aeolus*	16. *Eumaeus*
8. *Lestrygonians*	17. *Ithaca*
9. *Scylla & Charybdis*	18. *Penelope*

Other abbreviations for works frequently cited are:

Budgen   Frank Budgen, *James Joyce and the Making of 'Ulysses'*, London, 1934.

Ellmann   Richard Ellmann, *James Joyce*, New York, 1959.

Gorman   Herbert Gorman, *James Joyce*, New Edn., New York, 1948.

Letters   *Letters of James Joyce*, ed. Stuart Gilbert, New York, 1957.

Slocum   John J. Slocum and Herbert Cahoon, *A Bibliography of James Joyce, 1882–1941*, New Haven, 1953.

CONTENTS

I

THE DESIGN OF *ULYSSES*

1. GROWTH OF A MASTERPIECE

ALTHOUGH *Ulysses* bears the date-line 'Trieste-Zürich-Paris, 1914–1921' its origin lies in Joyce's early experiences, and a full history of its development would be a history of his artistic career to the age of forty. In 1917, with the novel well under way, Joyce told a Zürich friend, Georges Borach, of his early fascination with the *Odyssey*:

> I was twelve years old when we dealt with the Trojan War at school; only the *Odyssey* stuck in my memory. I want to be candid: at twelve I liked the mysticism in Ulysses. When I was writing *Dubliners*, I first wished to choose the title *Ulysses in Dublin*, but gave up the idea. In Rome, when I had finished about half of the *Portrait*, I realized that the Odyssey had to be the sequel, and I began to write *Ulysses*.[1]

The version of the *Odyssey* Joyce encountered at the age of twelve was Charles Lamb's *Adventures of Ulysses*, and the 'mysticism' that he liked was probably Lamb's fusing of realistic action and symbolism, his attempt—announced in the Preface—to make the characters both human figures and figures denoting 'external force or internal temptations'.[2] Lamb's 'mystical' view of the *Odyssey*, so unlike that of most nineteenth-century translators and critics, had a lasting influence on Joyce's imagination, proving to him that the Homeric plot could be recreated in the language of contemporary life and used as a foundation for symbolic actions. In 1922, shortly after the publication of *Ulysses*, he recommended that his Aunt Josephine (Mrs. William Murray) buy Lamb's *Adventures* as a guide to the novel, and every reader can profit from this advice.[3] In contrast to the Victorian *Odyssey* of Butcher and Lang, Lamb's version helps us to understand the many

1

similarities between the 'internal temptations' of Ulysses and those of Leopold Bloom.

But although Ulysses was a 'Favourite Hero' of the young Joyce,[4] the first evidence that he intended to write a story based on the wanderings of his hero dates from 1906, when he was twenty-four years old and working on *Dubliners*. On 30 September 1906 he wrote from Rome to his brother Stanislaus: 'I have a new story for *Dubliners* in my head. It deals with Mr Hunter [a Dublin jew reported to be a cuckold, later one of the models for Bloom]'. In November Joyce was still thinking of the story; then, on 6 February 1907, he notified Stanislaus that '*Ulysses* never got any forrader than the title'.[5] The extreme personal difficulties the Joyce family encountered while living in Rome were obviously responsible in part for this neglect of *Ulysses*, but a further reason for delay is suggested by Joyce's remarks to Georges Borach. During his stay in Rome (July 1906–March 1907) Joyce realized that a full-length work based on the *Odyssey* 'had to be the sequel' to *Portrait of the Artist* (then the half-completed *Stephen Hero*), and as a consequence the writing of the short story *Ulysses* was deferred. Additional evidence of this awakening to the possibilities of a modern 'epic' may be found in those parallels between *Dubliners* and the *Odyssey* which have been detected by some critics. It is significant that these parallels are most tenuous in *The Dead*, the only story written after Joyce had abandoned his plan to make *Ulysses* a part of *Dubliners* and had foreseen a sequel to his autobiographical novel.[6]

Late in 1907 Joyce told Stanislaus that he wished to expand his story *Ulysses* into a short book, 'a Dublin *Peer Gynt*'; it is not clear whether the short story was actually written at this time, or simply planned.[7] In any event nothing substantial came of the project, although between 1907 and 1914 Joyce maintained his interest in the *Odyssey*, carefully reading Homer and investigating the work of commentators such as Bérard.[8] He never lost sight of the potential 'sequel' to *A Portrait*, and several manuscript fragments have survived which link *Stephen Hero* and *A Portrait* with *Ulysses* (see Appendix B, where these fragments are described and analysed). Two of the fragments indicate that Joyce was working on a rudimentary version of the Martello tower scene while completing *Portrait*, but excluded it from his autobiographical novel in anticipation of the first chapter in *Ulysses*. These discarded passages show that the design of *Ulysses* was gradually developing in Joyce's mind while he completed *Portrait of the Artist*.

Early in 1914, with *Portrait* finished and appearing serially in the *Egoist*, Joyce turned his full attention to the problems of a sequel and began the monumental task which was to take him seven years. The total design of the new work was already far enough advanced in his mind that he could start by 'setting down' what Herbert Gorman describes as 'the preliminary sketches for the final sections'.[9] Undoubtedly he wished to clarify some general problems of structure before concentrating on the early episodes. The nature of these 'preliminary sketches' is difficult to determine, but presumably they contained material later included in the *Nostos* or close (the last three episodes). In June of 1920, with the *Circe* episode still unwritten, Joyce wrote to his literary agents, the English firm of Pinker & Son, that the 'close of the book' was 'already drafted'.[10] Less than a month later he expanded upon this statement in a letter to Harriet Shaw Weaver: 'A great part of the Nostos or close was written several years ago and the style is quite plain.'[11] The amount of the *Nostos* previously written can be surmised from a passage in a letter sent to Frank Budgen late in 1920:

I am going to leave the last word with Molly Bloom, the final episode being written through her thoughts and tired Poldy being then asleep. *Eumeus* you know so there remains only to think out Ithaca in the way I suggest.[12]

These remarks would seem to indicate that *Eumaeus* was the first part of the *Nostos* to be fully conceived and outlined.

Confirmation for this may be found in Gorman's statement that Joyce wrote *Circe* and *Eumaeus* 'simultaneously', work on the partially constructed *Eumaeus* being a relief from the complexities of the Nighttown episode.[13]

These early 'sketches for the final sections' raise the important question of the order in which Joyce wrote *Ulysses* and, later, *Finnegans Wake*. His approach to both works was 'pictorial'. In each case he attempted to visualize the general design of the work before completing individual episodes, and the process of composition did not correspond with the final order of the chapters; instead, he programmed his writing as his interests or the need for clarification dictated. He felt that only through a long process of revision and elaboration could a work of art achieve unified form. 'The elements needed will only fuse after a prolonged existence together', he wrote in defence of his painstaking method of composition.[14] For Joyce revision provided an opportunity for exploration and discovery; it was a search for form. While constructing *Ulysses* and *Finnegans Wake* he often worked on several sections at the same time, allowing the development of one to illuminate the problems of the others. This method was made possible, as we shall see later, by the unique form of Joyce's late work.

In the spring of 1914, with the 'preliminary sketches for the final sections' of *Ulysses* behind him, Joyce called a temporary halt to the planning of *Ulysses* and began work on his play, *Exiles*, which occupied a large portion of his time until late 1915.[15] The writing of *Exiles* seems to have provided Joyce with a catharsis that was necessary before he could fully develop the design of *Ulysses*. In *Exiles* he exorcised the spectre of Ibsen, a dominant influence since the days at University College; but, more important, he dramatized in the play a personal experience of sexual jealousy, thus preparing the way for objective treatment of Bloom's jealousy and cuckoldry.[16] The writing of *Exiles*, like Stephen's laughter in the Library episode, enabled Joyce to 'free his mind from his mind's bondage' (U 209).

4

Exiles completed, Joyce once again turned his full attention to *Ulysses* and began to compose the episodes in their final order, often working on two or three at once to promote their 'fusion'.[17] By June of 1915, when he and his family left Trieste for Zürich, he had begun the third episode, *Proteus*.[18] During the hard years of 1915 and 1916, while Joyce struggled for a living in the refugee city of Zürich, the writing of *Ulysses* still progressed. The design of the work seemed to exist as a single image in his mind, and no piece of information was too irrelevant to find its place in the comprehensive pattern.

As early as May of 1918 Joyce had conceived the basic structure of *Ulysses* in what was substantially its final form. On the 18th of that month he wrote to Harriet Weaver:

I thank you for having transmitted to me the kind proposal of my New York publisher. Will you please write to him and say that I could not, for many reasons, undertake to deliver the entire typescript of *Ulysses* during the coming autumn. If the *Little Review* continues to publish it regularly he may publish as a cheap paperbound book the *Telemachia*, that is, the three first episodes—under the title, *Ulysses I*. I suggest this in case his idea be to keep the few persons who read what I write from forgetting that I still exist. The second part, the *Odyssey*, contains eleven episodes. The third part, *Nostos*, contains three episodes. In all seventeen episodes of which, including that which is now being typed and will be sent in a day or two, *Hades*, I have delivered six. It is impossible to say how much of the book is really written. Several other episodes have been drafted for the second time but that means nothing because although the third episode of the *Telemachia* has been a long time in the second draft I spent about 200 hours over it before I wrote it out finally.[19]

By the end of 1918 the first seven episodes had been published by the *Little Review* in tentative versions, and by the beginning of 1920 serial publication had reached the *Cyclops* episode. Meanwhile, Joyce had got as far as the thirteenth episode, *Nausicaa*, in his writing, with parts of *Oxen of the Sun* and the *Nostos* already drafted and material for the other episodes collected. It was at this point, and while writing the last five episodes, that he undertook 'the great revision'. One is tempted to compare this recasting of the earlier episodes with Henry James's revision of his early novels and tales for the New York Edition, but I think there is an important difference. James's revisions were, for the most part, elaborations and refinements of elements already present in the earlier versions: they seem to be logical extensions of the original intent. But Joyce's late revisions—as we shall see later—often ran counter to the intent of his earlier work. The early episodes of *Ulysses* were drafted in a style not far from that of *A Portrait*; but when Joyce returned to them in 1920 and 1921 he attempted radical alterations in their style and structure. In October of 1921, with parts of the novel already in proof, he wrote to Harriet Weaver concerning these late revisions:

Eolus is recast. *Hades* and the *Lotus-eaters* much amplified and the other episodes retouched a good deal. Not much change has been made in the *Telemachia* (the first three episodes of the book).[20]

Joyce never stopped revising *Ulysses*, labouring unceasingly to give the novel a closer texture and more organic form. Every episode was subjected to an intensive process of revision; the extant drafts reveal massive alterations and augmentations. *Oxen of the Sun* and *Circe* seem to have given Joyce the most difficulty, as might be expected. 'I wrote the *Circe* Episode nine times from first to last', he told a friend in January of 1921.[21]

As in the final stages of his work on *Finnegans Wake*, Joyce continued to augment and correct episodes until the moment of publication. Usually five or more sets of proof were required. In protesting to John Quinn against the sale of the *Ulysses* manuscript to A. S. W. Rosenbach, Joyce said:

It must be understood, however, that I will not write in any pages of the MS. to 'complete' it. The additions were made by me on printed proofs.[22]

The surviving sets of proofs for *Ulysses* were copiously corrected, the 'emendations and additions exceeding sometimes 160 words on a single page'.[23] *Ulysses* provides a perfect illustration of Paul Valéry's remark that a work of art is never finished, but only abandoned.

The burden of the evidence is that *Ulysses* was written 'all of a piece'. Many of the later episodes were planned and drafted early in the course of composition, while the episodes from *Calypso* to *Nausicaa* were considerably reworked during the years 1919–21 so that they would harmonize with Joyce's evolving aesthetic ideals. In his final revisions, Joyce sought to invest the earlier and plainer episodes with a complexity and richness of technique commensurate with that found in *Circe*, *Ithaca* and *Oxen of the Sun*. If we except *Penelope*, a late-comer and structurally a post-script, one might almost say that Joyce began to write *Ulysses* from both ends at once, meeting in the *Circe* episode where all the motifs are drawn together and transformed.[24] This same strategy was used again in the making of *Finnegans Wake*, and Joyce acknowledged it in a conversation with his friend August Suter. 'I am boring through a mountain from two sides', he told Suter shortly after he began work on the *Wake*. 'The question is, how to meet in the middle'.[25]

2. THE LATE REVISIONS

The final stage in the growth of *Ulysses* marked a turning-point in Joyce's artistic development. It was during the last three years of composition (1919–21) that he wrote the intricate later episodes and revised the opening chapters, seeking to fuse the entire work into an organic whole. A close examination of the methods he employed at this time will demonstrate how far he had progressed from his earlier works, and will prepare the way for an understanding of those basic principles which governed the entire composition of *Finnegans Wake*.

By far the most extended and important descriptions of the manner in which Joyce constructed *Ulysses* are found in Frank

Budgen's *James Joyce and the Making of 'Ulysses'*. Budgen was an intimate friend, and his book is a faithful record of Joyce at work. His account of the methods Joyce employed in resolving the formal problems posed by *Ulysses* provides an antidote to the sententious analyses of later critics such as Stuart Gilbert, who tend to over-emphasize the superficial order of the novel. Here, as a starting point, is a long passage describing Joyce at work in 1918–19.

Joyce's method of composition always seemed to me to be that of a poet rather than that of a prose writer. The words he wrote were far advanced in his mind before they found shape on paper . . . he was a great believer in his luck. What he needed would come to him. That which he collected would prove useful in its time and place. And as, in a sense, the theme of *Ulysses* is the whole of life, there was no end to the variety of material that went to its building. Of the time detail of 1904 was none around him, but what he saw and heard in 1918 or 1919 would do just as well, for the shapes of life remain constant: only the dress and manners change. I have seen him collect in the space of a few hours the oddest assortment of material: a parody on the *House that Jack Built*, the name and action of a poison, the method of caning boys on training ships, the wobbly cessation of a tired unfinished sentence, the nervous trick of a convive turning his glass in inward-turning circles, a Swiss music-hall joke turning on a pun in Swiss dialect, a description of the Fitzsimmons shift.

In one of the richest pages of *Ulysses* Stephen, on the seashore, communing with himself and tentatively building with words, calls for his tablets. . . . As far as concerns the need for tablets, the self-portrait was still like, only in Zürich Joyce was never without them. And they were not library slips, but little writing blocks specially made for the waistcoat pocket. At intervals, alone or in conversation, seated or walking, one of these tablets was produced, and a word or two scribbled on it at lightning speed as ear or memory served his turn. No one knew how all this material was given place in the completed pattern of his work, but from time to time in Joyce's flat one caught glimpses of a few of those big orange-coloured envelopes that are one of the glories of Switzerland, and these I always took to be storehouses of building material. The method of making a multitude of criss-cross notes in pencil was a strange one for a man whose sight was never good. A necessary adjunct to the method was a huge oblong magnifying glass.[26]

Joyce laboured to a predetermined pattern; each fragment of material he gathered was marked for a specific place in the novel's general design. The entire work, with all its complex internal allusions, seems to have developed in Joyce's mind as a single vast 'image'. Consequently, as Budgen points out, the 'words he wrote were far advanced in his mind before they found shape on paper'.

Budgen's description naturally raises the question of how Joyce organized and preserved the diverse materials of his novel: the answer is that they were collected in abbreviated form on a variety of note-sheets. Silvio Benco, writing of Joyce's visit to Trieste in 1919–20, provides the first eye-witness account of these notes.

He showed me the loose sheets on which he prepared the material of each episode, notes as to composition, quotations, references, ideas, essays in various styles. When the rough material was ready, he devoted himself to writing out the complete episode, and this he usually did in less than a month. Following this method, *Ulysses* had been begun in Trieste before the war, continued in Zürich, and now resumed in Trieste.[27]

These sheets were, in all probability, the classified repository for the fragments of material mentioned by Budgen. A number of the *Ulysses* note-sheets which have survived are marked with the names of the episodes to which they refer, and even the undesignated ones are concerned primarily with a single episode.[28] Evidently Joyce would sort out his fragmentary notes according to episodes and then copy them on to foolscap sheets or into notebooks, gradually building up a list of additions and insertions for each chapter.

We have already noted the 'great revision' of earlier episodes which Joyce undertook while writing the final sections of his novel. Considering the complex patterns of association which

bind *Ulysses* together, it was natural that as the novel expanded
the author should wish to augment earlier chapters already
published in the *Egoist* and *Little Review*. But Joyce's revisions
went far beyond the alterations and additions of the conventional
novelist. The entire novel was re-shaped, technical emphases
were altered and a new aesthetic 'direction' introduced. The
remainder of this chapter will be primarily an assessment of this
new 'direction'.

Joyce's letters of 1920–21 illuminate his use of the accumulated notes for early and late episodes. In a letter to Harriet
Weaver, written on 12 July 1920, he commented on their
function:

My intention is to remain here [in Paris] three months in order to
write the last adventure *Circe* in peace (?) and also the first episode of
the close. For this purpose I brought with me a recast of my notes and
MS and also an extract of insertions for the first half of the book in case
it be set up during my stay here.[29]

Later in 1920 Joyce again referred to these accumulated notes,
in a letter to John Quinn:

I began *Ulysses* in 1914 and shall finish it, I suppose, in 1921. This
is, I think, the twentieth address at which I have written it—and the
coldest. The complete notes fill a small valise, but in the course of
continual changings very often it was not possible to sort them for the
final time before the publication of certain instalments [in the *Little
Review*]. The insertions (chiefly verbal or phrases, rarely passages)
must be put in for the book publication. Before leaving Trieste I did
this sorting for all episodes up to and including *Circe*. The episodes
which have the heaviest burden of addenda are *Lotus-eaters*, *Lestrygonians*, *Nausikaa* and *Cyclops*.[30]

These minor insertions mentioned by Joyce are consistent with
the type of addenda found on the *Ulysses* note-sheets. The
material of the note-sheets was used in an advanced stage of composition, either to augment an episode already in print or to
expand a manuscript draft.

A year later (7 October 1921), during the last weeks of the writing of *Ulysses*, Joyce elaborated upon the use of these accumulated insertions in a letter to Miss Weaver:

A few lines to let you know I am here again with MSS and pencils (red, green and blue) and cases of books and trunks and all the rest of my impedimenta nearly snowed up in proofs and nearly crazed with work. *Ulysses* will be finished in about three weeks, thank God, and (if the French printers don't all leap into the Rhône in despair at the mosaics I send them back) ought to be published early in November. I sent the *Penelope* episode to the printer as Larbaud wants to read it before he finishes his article for the Nouvelle Revue Française. The *Ithaca* episode which precedes it I am now putting in order. It is in reality the end as *Penelope* has no beginning, middle or end. I expect to have early next week about 240 pages of the book as it will appear ready and will send on. *Eolus* is recast. *Hades* and the *Lotus-eaters* much amplified and the other episodes retouched a good deal. Not much change has been made in the *Telemachia* . . .[31]

This is Joyce's first reference to the use of coloured pencils in the sorting process. While composing *Ulysses* he crossed out a number of notes in coloured pencil (usually red, blue, or green), either to indicate that these notes had been incorporated into the text or that he intended to use them at a certain stage in the process of composition. Although many of the notes slashed through in coloured pencil are not to be found in the finished novel, *none* of the uncrossed notes ever appear. I think one may safely conclude that Joyce transferred most of the lined-out notes either to a manuscript draft or a condensed list of insertions, but that many were eliminated in the last revisions. The function of the various colours is not completely clear: at times they indicate separate stages in the process of composition, while often they are used to differentiate among notes for two or more episodes appearing on the same sheet. For example, on a sheet where most of the notes are for *Ithaca* the insertions actually used in that episode are slashed in blue, while two notes which were used in the revision of earlier episodes are slashed in red.

Valery Larbaud, who began to write his famous article on *Ulysses* while Joyce was still revising the last sections of the novel, has described the note-sheets used by Joyce at that time.

It [Joyce's text] is a genuine example of the art of mosaic. I have seen the drafts. They are entirely composed of abbreviated phrases underlined in various-coloured pencil. These are annotations intended to recall to the author complete phrases; and the pencil-marks indicate according to their colour that the underlined phrase belongs to such or such an episode. It makes one think of the boxes of little coloured cubes of the mosaic workers.[32]

Larbaud's description obviously applies either to the note-sheets under discussion or to similar compilations of rough notes. However, I would disagree with his statement that Joyce inter-lined (a more accurate term than 'underlined') his notes in order to indicate their final positions in the novel; it seems more likely that they were crossed out at the time of their insertion into preliminary drafts of the episodes.

The comparison between Joyce's method of composition and that of the mosaic workers, which has been used by Budgen[33] as well as Larbaud, is strikingly appropriate. Joyce himself called the corrected galleys of *Ulysses* 'mosaics'.[34] He did not write *Ulysses* straight through, following the final order of the episodes. First it was necessary to determine the design of the novel, to visualize its characters and the course of the action, and this entailed putting scattered portions on paper in order to clarify them. Then, like the mosaic worker, Joyce collected and sorted material to fit the design. Finally, the fragments were placed in their proper positions through a process of rough drafts and revisions.

The evidence in favour of Joyce's having compiled and used the note-sheets late in the writing of *Ulysses* is substantial. The first mention of them is in the article by Silvio Benco previously cited, which refers to the period 1919–20; however, since comments by Joyce's friends on the years prior to 1918 are extremely rare, this carries little weight. More conclusive is the evidence of the notes themselves, most of which are of a nature that would occur in a late revision of the text: verbal insertions, cross-references, minor themes. Several of the notes can be assigned to a precise stage in the process of composition. The burden of this evidence is that the sheets were used (and probably compiled) sometime after 1919, when Joyce was writing the final episodes and augmenting the earlier ones. Many of the notes entered the text during the last-minute revisions of galley proof.

The typical note found on the *Ulysses* note-sheets is a minor verbal insertion designed to enrich the texture of the narrative. These verbal insertions are particularly common on the *Nausicaa*, *Penelope*, and—as might be expected—*Oxen of the Sun* sheets. The sentimental phrases for Gerty MacDowell's 'namby-pamby jammy marmalady drawersy ... style',[35] the multitudinous events and fragments of conversation recalled by Molly in her closing reverie, the characteristic phrases for one imitated style or another—entries such as these make up the body of the *Nausicaa*, *Penelope*, and *Oxen* sheets. The left-hand column below contains a series of phrases transcribed from an *Oxen* note-sheet. The word 'red' has been placed in square brackets after each phrase slashed by Joyce in red pencil; a heavy line indicates that one or more notes have been omitted. In the right-hand column are those sections from the opening of *Oxen of the Sun* affected by the notes, with the pertinent passages italicized. The first pages of *Oxen of the Sun* which appeared in the *Little Review* for September–December 1920 were included in the published novel without change; this suggests that Joyce wrote the later episodes of *Ulysses* directly into his final 'complex' style, then revised the earlier episodes to harmonize with them.

| a plan was by them adopted [red] | Certainly *in every public work* which in it anything of gravity contains preparation should be with importance commensurate and therefore *a plan was by them adopted* |

was provided valiantly [red]

---

in every public work it is to be considered [red]

terrestial orb [red]
with sapience endowed [red]

concealed from them were not

part of wisdom
what pertains to [red]
that no age be silent about your praises
not solely for the copiously moneyed [red]
scarcely or not even scarcely [red]
not sufficiently [red]

---

aspect of the most distracting spectacles [red]

(whether by having preconsidered or as the maturation of experience it is difficult in being said which the discrepant opinions of subsequent inquirers are not up to the present congrued to render manifest) whereby maternity was so far from all accident possibility removed that whatever care the patient in that allhardest of woman hour chiefly required and *not solely for the copiously opulent* but also for her who *not* being *sufficiently moneyed scarcely* and often *not even scarcely* could subsist *valiantly* and for an inconsiderable emolument *was provided* (U 378).

Universally that person's acumen is esteemed very little perceptive concerning whatsoever matters are being held as most profitably by mortals *with sapience endowed* to be studied ... (U 377).

Before born babe bliss had. Within womb won he worship. Whatever in that one case done commodiously done was. A couch by midwives attended with wholesome food reposeful cleanest swaddles as though forthbringing were now done and by wise foresight set: but to this no less of what drugs there is need and surgical implements which are *pertaining to* her case not omitting *aspect* of all very *distracting spectacles* in various latitudes by our *terrestrial orb* offered together with images, divine and human, the cogitation of which by sejunct females is to tumescence conducive or eases issue in the high sunbright wellbuilt fair home of mothers when, ostensibly far gone and reproductitive, it is come by her thereto to lie in, her term up (U 378).

All those notes which Joyce marked in red are found in the text, inserted almost without change. Their function in reinforcing the deliberately stilted and archaic dialect of the prelude to *Oxen* is obvious. The episode must have been far advanced in Joyce's mind when he made these notes, as they are all stylistic additions to a particular section of the narrative. This process of deliberately 'thickening' the existing narrative foreshadows the continuous revisions of *Work in Progress*, where the prose becomes denser and more complex with each successive revision.

Often the notes on a sheet bear little relation to each other except for the fact that they are intended for roughly the same part of an episode; take, for instance, this series of consecutive notes from a sheet labelled '*Ithaca*'.

a donkey & trap [blue]	. . . a donkey with wicker trap or smart phaeton with good working solidungular cob (roan gelding, 14h) (U 699).
pleasant reflectio[n]s produce sleep [blue]	What pleasant reflection accompanied this action? The reflection that . . . (U 707).
simple interest at 5% of—LB in tree (jew) [red]	In 1885 he . . . in support of his political convictions, had climbed up into a secure position amid the ramifications of a tree on Northumberland road . . . (U 701).
rabbitry [blue]	A rabbitry and fowlrun . . . (U 699).
baronial hall, groaning table [green]	Not to inherit . . . a baronial hall with gatelodge and carriage drive nor, on the other hand . . . (U 697).
MB spasm old clockface	
space reversible time no [green]	An unsatisfactory equation between an exodus and return in time through reversible space and an exodus and return in space through irreversible time (U 713).

Joyce's synthesizing mind brought these stray fragments of material together in the dry, factual catechism of *Ithaca*. Unlike the notes for *Oxen of the Sun* cited above, these were not collected with their exact positions in *Ithaca* already determined; Joyce only knew what episode he wished to include them in, and they were worked into the text as opportunities for their use arose. In this case the different colours of pencil probably represent different periods of revision, various drafts of the episode.

More often than not, however, a series of notes will have a thematic unity even though the passages founded upon it are scattered in the final text. A good illustration is the following group of notes from a *Circe* sheet, all of which are slashed in blue pencil.

Sweetly hoarsely	Boylan murmurs '*Sweetly, hoarsely*', Molly '*Hoarsely, sweetly*' in the scene on pp. 552–53 of *Ulysses*.
Kiss the whip	
Mrs. Bloom	'Mrs Bloom up yet?' Spoken to Bloom by Boylan (U 551).
last articles	Bloom replies to Boylan: 'I'm afraid not, sir, the last articles . . .' (U 551).
ask every 20 minutes	'Ask for that every ten minutes.' Bello to Bloom (U 522).
touches the spot	'Touches the spot?' Bello to Bloom (U 529).

All these references are related to the scene where Bloom imagines himself assisting Blazes Boylan in his adulterous affair with Molly (U 551–53), and thus to the theme of male impotence. 'Sweetly hoarsely', 'Mrs. Bloom', and 'last articles' are used in the same scene. 'Ask every 20 minutes' and 'touches the spot' appear—slightly transformed—in that section of *Circe* where

Bella, metamorphosed into a male figure (Bello), dominates the female aspects of Bloom's personality (U 518ff.).

BELLO

Ask for that every ten minutes. Beg, pray for it as you never prayed before. (*He thrusts out a figged fist and foul cigar.*) Here, kiss that. Both. Kiss. (*He throws a leg astride and, pressing with horseman's knees, calls in a hard voice.*) Gee up! A cockhorse to Banbury cross. I'll ride him for the Eclipse stakes . . . (U 522).

The allusion to 'Ride a cockhorse' points forward to Bloom's hallucinated vision of Boylan visiting Molly, where Lydia Douce cries: 'Yumyum. O, he's carrying her round the room doing it! Ride a cock horse' (U 552). The theme of Bloom's impotence, his sexual 'eclipse', is introduced again several pages after Bello rides him 'for the Eclipse stakes'. In the passage which incorporates the last note in the sequence ('touches the spot'), Bello derides Bloom as an inadequate cuckold (U 529).

The note not found in the published text of *Ulysses*, 'Kiss the whip', is undoubtedly another reference to Bloom's impotence in the presence of more virile males. Perhaps it does reach the text, in a slightly changed form, when Bello '*thrusts out a figged fist and foul cigar*' to Bloom and says: 'Here, kiss that. Both. Kiss' (U 522).

This grouping of related notes is typical of the *Ulysses* note-sheets. Although sometimes the notes on a sheet have no unity beyond the fact that they were gathered for a particular episode, more often Joyce assembled his material by themes and motifs, ultimately incorporating the notes into one or more scenes in the finished text. In this manner he achieved an extraordinary structural unity through a network of cross-references.

In compiling the note-sheets Joyce employed a form of associational shorthand to record the outlines of passages already visualized. A sequence such as 'exhalations, see breath, telegraph wires', jotted down for *Ithaca* but never used, is characteristic:

the words indicate an associational development that could form the basis of an extended passage. Similar cryptic patterns are found in Joyce's notes for *Exiles*, accompanied by elaborate explanations which are some indication of the vast amount of organized material represented by the abbreviated notes for *Ulysses*. For example, the skeleton sequence 'Blister-amber-silver-oranges-apples-sugarstick-hair-spongecake-ivy-roses-ribbon' is explained by Joyce as follows:

The blister reminds her of the burning of her hand as a girl. She sees her own amber hair and her mother's silver hair. This silver is the crown of age but also the stigma of care and grief which she and her lover have laid upon it. This avenue of thought is shunned completely; and the other aspect, amber turned to silver by the years, her mother a prophecy of what she may one day be is hardly glanced at. Oranges, apples, sugarstick—these take the place of the shunned thoughts and are herself as she was, being her girlish joys. Hair: the mind turning again to this without adverting to its colour, adverting only to a distinctive sexual mark and to its growth and mystery rather than to its mystery. The softly growing symbol of her girlhood. Spongecake; a weak flash again of joys which now begin to seem more those of a child than those of a girl. Ivy and roses: she gathered ivy often when out in the evening with girls. Roses grew then a sudden scarlet note in the memory which may be a dim suggestion of the roses of the body. The ivy and the roses carry on and up, out of the idea of growth, through a creeping vegetable life into ardent perfumed flower life the symbol of mysteriously growing girlhood, her hair. Ribbon for her hair. Its fitting ornament for the eyes of others, and lastly for his eyes. Girlhood becomes virginity and puts on 'the snood that is the sign of maidenhood'. A proud and shy instinct turns her mind away from the loosening of her bound-up hair—however sweet or longed for or inevitable—and she embraces that which is hers alone and not hers and his also—happy distant dancing days, distant, gone forever, dead, or killed?[36]

Joyce used the associational technique which governs this passage in two ways: (1) to order the impressions and memories of his characters, and (2) to organize the heterogeneous raw materials of his art.

Often the most suggestive words or phrases on the note-sheets are elements in the 'internal monologue' of a character, as in this sequence from a sheet containing notes for several episodes:

It seems history is to blame, nightmare. God noise in street, never let jews in, O'Rourke, left goal, Pyrrhus, Helen.

This is a recapitulation of the central elements around which Stephen's mind is oriented in the *Nestor* episode; he is haunted by memories of them for the remainder of the day, and they reappear again and again in his thoughts. In this note Joyce was reminding himself in capsule form of a scene to be kept fresh in Stephen's memory.

Many of the notes for *Ulysses* are 'shorthand' notes in the sense that they were aimed at reminding Joyce of a fuller version already visualized. Expansion and elaboration are the most significant characteristics of Joyce's revisions. Often in the *Ithaca* episode an entire question-and-answer passage is the development of a single short note: the question 'What pleasant reflection accompanied this action?' and its answer (U 707) can be traced to the abbreviated 'pleasant reflections produce sleep'. At their most elaborate the notes are merely rough outlines of the final version:

£5 reward, missing gent aged about 40 height 5, 8, full build, dark complexion, may have since grown a beard. Was dressed when last seen. Above will be paid for his discovery.
(From an *Ithaca* note-sheet)

£5 reward lost, stolen or strayed from his residence 7 Eccles street, missing gent about 40, answering to the name of Bloom, Leopold (Poldy), height 5 ft 9½ inches, full build, olive complexion, may have since grown a beard, when last seen was wearing a black suit. Above sum will be paid for information leading to his discovery (U 712).

Details such as name, address, and colour of suit, the standard components of a 'missing persons' notice, would have been superfluous in a note made by Joyce for his own use; they could be added later. Also added when he expanded the note were the suggestions of a 'strayed animal' advertisement: 'lost, stolen or strayed' and 'answering to the name of Bloom'.

The most interesting of Joyce's notes are those which illuminate the structure of the novel or the techniques of the various episodes. In the note-sheets he commonly refers to his characters by the names of their counterparts in the *Odyssey*. This is particularly noticeable on the *Eumaeus* sheets, where the Homeric allusions are richer than anywhere else. There are two possible reasons for this concentration in *Eumaeus*: (1) the episode was the first of the later chapters to be drafted, and Joyce seems to have relied more heavily on his Homeric parallels during the early stages of composition; (2) since the style of the episode is fatigued and murky to correspond with the moods of Bloom and Stephen, Joyce may have felt acutely the need for a supporting mythic structure.

However, only a fraction of the Homeric correspondences collected on the note-sheets appear in the text. In the following series, typical of the *Eumaeus* sheets, only four out of the eleven notes are slashed in pencil, and of these the only one I can definitely locate in *Ulysses* is non-Homeric: 'Enoch Arden Face at the Window' (see U 608). Two others, 'Ul. loses way in maze' and 'Ul. wants to try wife first', apply roughly to the final version of the episode.

> Ph. cease to convoy [slate gray]
> Ul. loses way in maze [blue]
> Pallos boosts her help
> Ul. denies, upbraids her
> She didn't want row with Neptune
> Ul. wants to try wife first [slate gray]
> Enoch Arden Face at the Window [slate gray]
> Ul. recognises Ithaca
> Kisses earth, shamrock clod
> Pallos & Ul. hide treasure
> Suitors 3 years round Pen

This series of notes served as a reminder of possible parallels between Bloom's return to Eccles Street and Ulysses' return to Ithaca. The first entry may refer to Joyce's acceptance of Victor Bérard's theory that the *Odyssey* is a 'hellenization' of the 'log' of a seafaring Semite, probably a Phoenician.[37] Ulysses is referred to as a Phoenician jew several times on the note-sheets.

The many Homeric parallels not included in the final text of *Ulysses* are significant, since they illustrate how much more important the Homeric background was for Joyce than it is to the reader. Invaluable to Joyce as a ready-made guide for the ordering of his material, the correspondences with the *Odyssey* do not provide a major level of meaning in the completed work. Ezra Pound was right in his early judgment of the Homeric framework: 'These correspondences are part of Joyce's mediaevalism and are chiefly his own affair, a scaffold, a means of construction, justified by the result, and justifiable by it only.'[38]

Among the notes which Joyce did *not* use, there are a number that shed light upon the novel's hidden relationships. For example, an unused note for *Penelope* illustrates the physiological basis of that episode: 'rose-menses'. Here the rose is a symbol of Molly's first love, the rose she wore in her hair 'like the Andalusian girls' when she was 'a Flower of the mountain' at Gibraltar (U 768); it is also the Rose of the Court of Love. But in Joyce's mind the rose was explicitly associated with menstruation.

The single word 'Comus', found on one of the *Circe* note-sheets, illuminates Joyce's attitude toward the temptations of Nighttown: evidently he associated Bella Cohen with the evil tempter in *Comus*, Bloom and Stephen with the virtuous brothers. There is a striking parallel between the Comus myth and the story of Circe's temptations in the *Odyssey*. According to Milton, Comus was the son of Bacchus and Circe; and the herb Haemony, which is given to the brothers by the Attendant Spirit and protects them from evil, is analogous to the 'Moly' Mercury gives

Ulysses. Joyce must once have intended to include the Comus story as a minor motif in the *Circe* episode.

In a series of unused notes for *Oxen of the Sun* the following equation occurs: 'Rudy=Mulvey'. This coupling of Bloom's dead son with the young naval officer who was Molly's first lover adds a new ironic dimension to his grief. Similarly, a new parallel for the paternal relationship between Bloom and Stephen is given in the equation 'Ul=W. Tell.', an unused note for *Ithaca*. Bloom, like William Tell, is the hero of an oppressed race, guided by love for his son.

Not only does the figure of Molly's first lover merge with the memory of her dead son, but Bloom sees his daughter Milly in Gerty MacDowell, the young girl on the beach in the *Nausicaa* episode: 'Milly Nausikaa' appears in one of the unused notes for the episode. Bloom, like Earwicker after him, is unconsciously in love with his own daughter as a young reincarnation of his wife, and for this reason he is attracted to the 'seaside' girl Gerty. Another reason to associate Nausicaa—Gerty with Milly is found in the latter's letter to Bloom, where she mentions Blazes Boylan's 'song about those seaside girls' (U 66).

The union of Bloom and Stephen in *Eumaeus* is mentioned in a note for the episode: 'Ul & Tel exchange unity.' The note is crossed in blue pencil, a sign that Joyce found an adequate expression for this interchange. The catechism of *Ithaca* opens with a closely related question-and-answer:

What parallel courses did Bloom and Stephen follow returning? Starting united both at normal walking pace . . . (U 650).

Joyce's exactitude in the use of concrete details and his dependence upon actual data, not so much for verisimilitude as for the satisfaction of his own scrupulous sense of artistic integrity, are illustrated by the rough map of Gibraltar which appears on one of the *Penelope* note-sheets. In order to refer accurately to Molly Bloom's birthplace, a city he had never visited, Joyce copied the important geographical points from a map and marked them on a sketch of his own. This sketch, which he obviously kept before him during the writing of the episode, includes a number of places mentioned by Molly in her closing monologue: 'windmill hill' (U 747), 'Europa point' (746 & 760), 'firtree cove' (746 & 745), 'OHaras tower' (745), 'Catalan bay' (750), and the 'Alameda gardens' (741, 747 & 768). Joyce constructed each of the episodes with the same regard for realistic detail. Frank Budgen records that he 'wrote the *Wandering Rocks* with a map of Dublin before him on which were traced in red ink the paths of the Earl of Dudley and Father Conmee. He calculated to a minute the time necessary for his characters to cover a given distance of the city'.[39]

Joyce was always scrupulously accurate in his descriptions of Dublin. In 1920 he wrote to his aunt Josephine Murray asking for details of the steps and trees at the Star of the Sea church in Sandymount, the scene of the *Nausicaa* episode.[40] Apparently such inquiries were not unusual. The next year he wrote the same aunt asking her to confirm the possibility of Bloom's letting himself down into the area-way of 7 Eccles Street:

Is it possible for an ordinary person to climb over the area railings of no 7 Eccles street, either from the path or the steps, lower himself down from the lowest part of the railings till his feet are within 2 feet or 3 of the ground and drop unhurt. I saw it done myself but by a man of rather athletic build. I require this information in detail in order to determine the wording of a paragraph.[41]

In all his work Joyce depended upon the concrete details of the Dublin of his youth, whether collected by himself or others. His many notebooks, the *Epiphanies*, the notes for *Dubliners* and *Stephen Hero* printed by Gorman in his biography, the *Ulysses* note-sheets—all are evidence of this naturalistic foundation. It was inherent in Joyce's notion of 'epiphany', the 'showing forth' of character through a seemingly trivial action or detail of appearance, that he would need particular facts about the men and women who sat for his characters. However, his insatiable desire for concrete details—especially the minutiae of setting—went far beyond the actual needs of his art. His obsessive concern with realistic detail reveals his desperate need for principles of order and authority. Deprived of social and religious order by his self-imposed exile, and acutely aware of the disintegrating forces in modern European society, Joyce turned to the concrete details of place and character as one stable base for his writing. Like the elaborate ordering principles discussed by Stuart Gilbert in his *James Joyce's 'Ulysses'*, the effects of which are manifest on every note-sheet, the details of Dublin life in 1904 were vastly important to Joyce during the making of *Ulysses*; but they are not essential to an understanding of the finished work. In so far as they obscure the central concerns of the novel they represent the price Joyce had to pay for his personal decisions.

The way in which the note-sheets kept the diverse elements of the novel clear in Joyce's mind is revealed in the handling of minor characters. Half of a double sheet containing notes for the *Circe* and *Cyclops* episodes is divided into squares numbered from 1 to 16, and under the appropriate numbers are listed the characters and a few of the important motifs introduced in each episode up to and including *Circe*. Not all the characters listed are of the living: 'Rudy' appears under *Hades* because of his presence in Bloom's thoughts during the funeral. Similarly, 'Elijah' and 'Parallax' are two of the 'characters' listed for *Lestrygonians*, and 'Cranly' is a character in *Telemachus*. Since the table ends with an abbreviated enumeration of the characters in *Circe*, it is logical to suppose that it was compiled sometime in 1920, while Joyce was working on that episode. Most of the names on the sheet are slashed through in either blue or red pencil, although 'Cranly', 'Rudy' and 'Parallax' are uncrossed. Perhaps Joyce wished to remember all the characters introduced in *Ulysses* prior to *Circe* so that he could be sure of incorporating them into that episode, where most of the novel's characters are brought together through the technique of metamorphosis.

Often it is possible to watch one of the novel's major motifs taking form on the note-sheets. While composing *Circe*, Joyce was constantly on the alert for analogies to 'Moly', the magic herb of Mercury that gave Ulysses protection against Circe's wiles. First and most important the talisman is Molly herself, Bloom's constant love for his wife. But around this central identification Joyce constructed a network of correspondences including both physical objects and qualities of Bloom's personality. He jotted down equivalents for 'Moly' as they came to him, and six different note-sheets yield an impressive list of the qualities and circumstances which save Bloom from the temptations of Bella Cohen's house and the fantasies of his own mind.

> Moly=absinthe, mercury [blue]
> Moly=chastity
> Chance=Moly (narrow shoes) [blue]
> Moly—indifference [blue]
> Moly—beauty [blue]
> Moly—laughter [blue]
> Moly—satire [blue]
> Moly=conscience [blue]
> Moly=escape from poison [blue]
> Moly (Met-salt)

Speaking of the difficulty Joyce had in finding equivalents for 'Moly', Frank Budgen comments:

'Moly' was a harder nut to crack. What was the herb that conferred upon Ulysses immunity from Circe's magic, and thus enabled him to be of service to his companions? What was the 'Moly' that saved Bloom from a surrender of his humanity? As a physical symbol Bloom's potato prophylactic against rheumatism and plague, inherited from his mother, would serve, but the real saviour of Bloom was a spiritual 'Moly', a state of mind. Joyce wrote to me in 1920: 'Moly is the gift of Hermes, god of public ways, and is the invisible influence (prayer, chance, agility, *presence of mind*, power of recuperation which saves in case of accident. This would cover immunity from syphilis—

swine love). . . . In this special case his plant may be said to have many leaves, indifference due to masturbation, pessimism congenital, a sense of the ridiculous, sudden fastidiousness in some detail, experience.'[42]

The many 'leaves' of 'Moly' enumerated on the note-sheets are similar to those mentioned by Joyce in his letter to Budgen. The only mysterious entry is 'Moly (Met-salt)', and the simplest explanation of it is that Joyce intended to introduce common table salt as a physical equivalent for 'Moly'. 'Met' probably stands for 'metamorphosis', the technique governing this identification and the entire episode as well.

Most of Joyce's notes which are not mere verbal insertions are reminders of motifs to be introduced or further developed. These notes, usually only a few words, were intended to remind Joyce of complex patterns of association already visualized and marked for specific positions in the narrative structure. The many notes on 'Moly' provide a good example of this, although they are concerned primarily with one episode. A phrase slashed in red pencil on one of the *Circe* sheets, '3 Legs of Man', indicates the way in which these notes could represent a theme or motif running through several episodes. The heraldic device of the Isle of Man is the 'Three Legs of Man', three flexed legs joined at the thighs, and the entry on the note-sheet refers specifically to that point in the Nighttown episode when the '*End of the World, a twoheaded octopus in gillie's kilts*', appears '*in the form of the Three Legs of Man*' (U 496). However, the Isle of Man is introduced in *Ulysses* as early as the *Hades* chapter through the figure of Reuben J. Dodd, solicitor and money-lender (U 92–93). Bloom tells his companions that Reuben's son dived into the Liffey to avoid being sent to the Isle of Man and away from the girl he loved. The scene in *Hades* establishes the Isle of Man as a symbol of isolation and sterility, and this central meaning is elaborated upon during succeeding episodes. Joyce's entry on the *Circe* sheet was simply a reminder that the emblem of the Isle of Man should appear in that episode as a climax to the chain of associations begun in the *Hades* chapter. It was the function of the note-sheets to assure that patterns and relationships already visualized by Joyce reached their fore-ordained positions in the text. Like the mosaic worker, he was continuously sorting and re-grouping his raw materials, assigning each fragment to its proper place in the general design. The mechanical nature of this process emphasizes the mechanical nature of those ordering principles which give *Ulysses* its superficial unity, and which sometimes obscure the deeper unity of the novel.

Joyce's revisions during the last three years of the making of *Ulysses* were so extensive that we must consult the earlier drafts if we are to view his artistic development in perspective. Any comprehensive treatment of *Ulysses* as a 'work in progress' would involve detailed analysis of the many stages of development through which each episode passed, and would go far beyond the scope of this study. Indeed, Joyce's revisions were so extensive, and his elaborations so complex, that only someone intimately familiar with the novel and its intricate career can fully comprehend them.[43] Fortunately, however, Joyce's methods of composition remained constant from episode to episode, and only a few examples are needed to illustrate the pattern of his late work on *Ulysses*. I shall cite three passages at this point, and several others in subsequent chapters; more would be redundant. These passages, in connection with the previous discussion of the notesheets, should convey a clear impression of the direction taken by Joyce's technical development during the period 1919–21.

The following passage of chauvinistic rhetoric, taken from an early draft of the *Cyclops* episode, is spoken by the pseudo-patriot Michael Cusack, known in the final version simply as 'the citizen'. It should be compared with the later version from the *Little Review* (Dec. 1919–Jan. 1920) printed immediately after it. The final version (U 320–22) is too long to be quoted in full, but it continues the process of elaboration evident in the *Little Review* version.

—Blatherskite, says Cusack. Can you point to any other part of the wide world where the population has decreased to fifty per cent in fifty years under a civilized government? Where are the thirty millions of Irish should be her today instead of four? Where are our potteries and textiles, the finest in the world? Look at the beds of the Barrow and Shannon they won't deepen. Where is the other civilized government would leave us as treeless as Portugal with a million acres of marsh & bog to make us all die of consumption? Not a ship to be seen in our harbours, Queenstown, Kinsale, Galway, Killybegs, the third biggest harbour in the whole world. We had our trade with Spain and Europe before they were born and with the Flemings too. We had Spanish ale & wine in Galway, the winebark on the widedark waterway. First, they tried to slaughter us all, then to banish us, then to make us paupers and to starve us in the penal days, then to buy us as they buy everything else (when all fruit fails welcome haws) but they're as far off now as they were 700 years ago when they first came here and damnation well they know. But they'll know more than that and to their cost when the first Irish battleship is seen breasting the waves with the green flag at her helm.[44]

★   ★   ★   ★

—*Raimeis,* says the citizen. Where are the twenty millions of Irish should be here today instead of four? And our potteries and textiles, the best in the world! And the beds of the Barrow and Shannon they won't deepen with a million acres of marsh and bog to make us all die of consumption.

—As treeless as Portugal we'll be soon, says John Wyse, if something is not [done] to reafforest the land. Larches, firs, all the trees of the conifer family are going fast. I was reading a report. . . .

—Save them, says the citizen, save the trees of Ireland for the future men of Ireland on the fair hills of Eire, O.

—Europe has its eyes on you, says Lenehan.

The fashionable international world attended en masse this afternoon at the wedding of the chevalier Jean Wyse de Nolan, grand high chief ranger of the Irish National Foresters, with Miss Fir Conifer of Pine Valley. The bride looked exquisitely charming in a creation of green mercerised silk, moulded on an underslip of gloaming grey, sashed with a yoke of broad emerald and finished with a triple flounce of darker hued fringe, the scheme being relieved by bretelles and hip insertions of acorn bronze. The maids of honour, Miss Larch Conifer and Miss Spruce Conifer, sisters of the bride, wore very becoming costumes in the same tone, a dainty *motif* of plume rose being worked into the pleats in a pinstripe and repeated capriciously in the jadegreen toques in the form of heron feathers of paletinted coral.

—And our eyes are on Europe, says the citizen. We had our trade with Spain and the French and with the Flemings before those mongrels were pupped. Spanish ale in Galway, the winebark on the winedark waterway.

—And will again, says Joe.

—And with the help of the holy mother of God we will again, says the citizen. Our harbours that are empty will be full again, Queenstown, Kinsale, Galway, Killybegs, the third largest harbour in the wide world. And will again, says he, when the first Irish battleship is seen breasting the waves with the green flag to the fore.[45]

The general pattern of revision that can be deduced from these versions of the *Cyclops* passage holds true for most of Joyce's late work on *Ulysses*. Three points should be noted:

(1) Although a selective process is still discernible, Joyce searching for the *mot juste* and attempting to record with absolute fidelity the speech rhythms of his characters, the majority of the revisions are *expansive* in nature. The original version provides a general outline of the situation, and establishes the realistic foundations; then, by a process of elaboration or accretion, this original outline is filled in and amplified.

(2) Almost every major element in the final version can be traced to some 'seed' in the original draft. Joyce followed a conventional process of association in expanding these 'seeds'.

(3) The formal 'correspondences' which characterize each episode of *Ulysses* and are carefully tabulated in Stuart Gilbert's study (in this case the technique of 'gigantism' and the inserted parodies) are usually a result of Joyce's late work on the episode. Here the elaborate parody of the coniferous wedding stems from a single sentence in the first version, the citizen's complaint that Ireland has been left 'as treeless as Portugal'.

The tendency of Joyce's late revisions is apparent in the growth of a short passage from the *Nausicaa* episode. Three stages in its development are reflected in a notebook which dates from 1919–1920.[46] Here is the original version:

A lonely lost candle climbed the air and broke and shed a cluster of violet and one white stars. They floated fell: and they faded. And among the elms a hoisted lintstock lit the lamp at Leahy's terrace. Twittering the bat flew here and there.

Subsequent marginal insertions and interlinear changes produced this expanded text:

A lost long candle wandered the sky from Mirus bazaar in aid of Mercer's hospital and broke drooping and shed a cluster of violet and one white stars. They floated fell: they faded. And among the elms a hoisted lintstock lit the lamp at Leahy's terrace. Twittering the bat flew here and there.

Another marginal note, apparently of a later date than the others, introduced the following sentence after 'Leahy's terrace':

By the screens of lighted window, by equal gardens a shrill voice went crying plaintively: *Evening Telegraph, extra edition Result of the Gold Cup races* and from the door of Dignam's house a boy ran out and called

Finally, after several more revisions, the passage reached *Ulysses* in this form:

A lost long candle wandered up the sky from Mirus bazaar in search of funds for Mercer's hospital and broke, drooping, and shed a cluster of violet but one white stars. They floated, fell: they faded. The shepherd's hour: the hour of holding: hour of tryst. From house to house, giving his everwelcome double knock, went the nine o'clock postman, the glowworm's lamp at his belt gleaming here and there through the laurel hedges. And among the five young trees a hoisted lintstock lit the lamp at Leahy's terrace. By screens of lighted windows, by equal gardens a shrill voice went crying, wailing: *Evening Telegraph, stop-press edition! Result of the Gold Cup race!* and from the door of Dignam's house a boy ran out and called. Twittering the bat flew here, flew there (U 372).

The growth of this passage provides a beautiful illustration of Joyce's method. Principles of artistic selection are still at work, and Joyce's care for the rhythm of his prose is everywhere evident. The alteration of 'elms' to 'five young trees' intensifies our visual sense of place; 'flew here, flew there' is greatly superior to 'flew here and there' as a description of the bat's darting flight. The search for the *mot juste* is reflected in the first sentence, where Joyce rejected 'climbed' and then 'ascended' before choosing 'wandered' as the correct equivalent for the candle's motion. All these changes are reminiscent of a conversation recorded by Frank Budgen:

I enquired about *Ulysses*. Was it progressing?
'I have been working hard on it all day', said Joyce.
'Does that mean that you have written a great deal?' I said.
'Two sentences', said Joyce.
I looked sideways but Joyce was not smiling. I thought of Flaubert.
'You have been seeking the *mot juste*?' I said.
'No', said Joyce. 'I have the words already. What I am seeking is the perfect order of words in the sentence. There is an order in every way appropriate. I think I have it'.
'What are the words?' I asked.
'I believe I told you', said Joyce, 'that my book is a modern Odyssey. Every episode in it corresponds to an adventure of Ulysses. I am now writing the *Lestrygonians* episode, which corresponds to the adventure of Ulysses with the cannibals. My hero is going to lunch. But there is a seduction motive in the Odyssey, the cannibal king's daughter. Seduction appears in my book as women's silk petticoats hanging in a shop window. The words through which I express the effect of it on my hungry hero are: "Perfume of embraces all him assailed. With hungered flesh obscurely, he mutely craved to adore." You can see for yourself in how many different ways they might be arranged'.[47]

But although Joyce maintained the care for rhythm and precision of phrasing that characterized his earlier revisions of *Dubliners* and *A Portrait*, his late work on *Ulysses* was primarily elaborative, the accretion of motifs and the addition of intricate ordering patterns. The major changes in the passage from *Nausicaa* are expansive rather than selective. The addition of the reference to Mirus bazaar connects the passage with several others in *Ulysses*; and the alteration of 'in aid of' to 'in search of funds for' accomplishes a slight change in our view of the enterprise.[48] Another addition, the sentence describing the rounds of the 'nine o'clock postman', not only reinforces the tone of the passage but establishes the hour, an essential part of Joyce's elaborate *schema*. However, the most important expansion involves the Gold Cup race, one of the novel's important *leitmotifs*. Bloom's accidental involvement with the race has become part of his sense of alienation; moreover, the victory of 'Throwaway' over 'Sceptre' may be seen symbolically as a defeat for fertility. Bringing with it this double sense of social and sexual frustration, the motif is ideally suited for this point in the *Nausicaa* episode, when Bloom's mind is filled with thoughts of Molly, Blazes Boylan, and his recent onanism.

In the evolution of this passage from *Nausicaa* we see how Joyce managed to unify *Ulysses* through a network of interlocking motifs and cross-references. Like a mosaic worker, he began with the basic outlines of his work and elaborated upon them, gradually establishing through a succession of detailed additions the extraordinary symbolic and realistic unity of the novel. In a sense the process of composition parallels the process which we follow as readers: a gradual accretion of details which finally form themselves into related patterns. To trace the evolution of an episode is to re-enact our own gradual apprehension of the work.

One more example of Joyce's method is needed to reinforce my point, this time an extract from Leopold Bloom's interior monologue in *Nausicaa*. Only the first and last versions are printed, omitting several intermediate stages of revision. In the final text I have italicized all those phrases or sentences which are present in some form in the original version.

That's very strange about my watch. Wonder is there any magnetic influence between the person because half past four was about the time he. Yes, I suppose, at once. Half past I remember looking in Pill lane. Also that now is magnetism. Dress up and look and suggest and let you see and see more and defy you if you're a man to see that, legs, look, look. and. Tip. Have to let fly.[49]

* * * *

Very strange about my watch. Wristwatches are always going wrong. *Wonder is there any magnetic influence between the person because that was about the time he. Yes, I suppose at once.* Cat's away the mice will play. *I remember looking in Pill lane. Also that now is magnetism.* Back of everything magnetism. Earth for instance pulling this and being pulled. That causes movement. And time? Well that's the time the movement takes. Then if one thing stopped the whole ghesabo would stop bit by bit. Because it's arranged. Magnetic needle tells you what's going on in the sun, the stars. Little piece of steel iron. When you hold out the fork. Come. Come. Tip. Woman and man that is. Fork and steel. Molly, he. *Dress up and look and suggest and let you see and see more and defy you if you're a man to see that and, like a sneeze coming, legs, look, look and if you have any guts in you. Tip. Have to let fly* (U 367).

Here the expansive nature of Joyce's late revisions is clearly revealed. The original version is almost a shorthand record of Bloom's associative process; successive revisions gave substance to these associations and bound together the themes of magnetism, time, and sexual attraction. At the same time, minor alterations and additions enhanced the characteristic idiom of Bloom's thoughts. The evolution of the passage exemplifies that 'slow elaborative patience' which the young Stephen thought 'classical', and which is the hallmark of Joyce's mature method.[50]

3. ORDER

It was inevitable that *Ulysses* should undergo extensive revision and elaboration as Joyce prepared the novel for final publication. Substantial changes in the earlier episodes were necessitated by the introduction in later chapters of new motifs and further details of characterization. Furthermore, Joyce's aesthetic ideals were considerably altered while *Ulysses* was 'in progress', and in the last stage of composition he sought to harmonize the form of the earlier episodes with the complexity he had achieved in drafting later sections. His method of characterization, which depended upon the accretion of thousands of minor details, meant that no section was ever 'finished'. The search for internal consistency and harmony was unending.

However, Joyce's reworking of the earlier sections went far beyond these predictable expansions and alterations. When one reads the versions of the early episodes published between 1918 and 1920 in the *Egoist* and *Little Review* one is struck immediately by the absence of many of those elaborate 'correspondences' documented by Stuart Gilbert and outlined by Joyce on a chart he circulated among his friends.[51] The familiar *schema* of the novel—the correspondence of each episode to a particular organ, colour, symbol, and art, and the casting of each episode in a distinctive style—is absent from the earlier versions. One of Joyce's major aims in revising the earlier episodes of *Ulysses* was to impose this elaborate pattern of correspondences upon them, to transform the entire novel into an 'epic' work.

By the time Joyce had reached mid-point in the drafting of *Ulysses* (*c.* 1919) the 'correspondences' for each episode were in the foreground of his mind. They are referred to constantly in his notes, and he was obviously conscious of them in the final stages of composition. While working on the *Oxen of the Sun* episode, which takes place in a Lying-In hospital during the birth of a child, Joyce consulted an elaborate chart which recorded the characteristics of the human foetus at every stage in its development.[52] This enabled him, while working on the episode, to establish correspondences involving the growth of the foetus, the evolution of the English language, the geological development of the earth, and the progress of *Ulysses* up to that point.[53] This

34

complex scheme was gradually woven into the episode and became an integral part of its substance: indeed, it *is* the substance. But when Joyce returned to the earlier episodes and attempted to impose similar schemes upon them, he was less successful. I think this accounts for the impression most of us have while reading *Ulysses* that many of the 'correspondences' in the earlier sections lie on the surface and hardly participate in the essential life of the episodes.

When one views the making of *Ulysses* in perspective, it is seen to embody Joyce's entire development from the techniques of *Dubliners* and *A Portrait* to those of *Finnegans Wake*. The earliest versions of the opening episodes were composed in the manner he employed while transforming *Stephen Hero* into *Portrait of the Artist*; but the principles which governed his work in 1920 and 1921 did not differ greatly from those he followed in writing *Finnegans Wake*. Anyone versed in the methods of the *Wake* will find the late elaborations of *Ulysses* familiar ground. During the writing of *Ulysses* Joyce's techniques and aesthetic ideals underwent a profound change. Of course one can argue—and with some justification—that the extreme techniques Joyce employed in finishing *Ulysses* are foreshadowed in the style and structure of his earlier works. But the notion of a technical revolution seems closer to the truth than that of evolution, for in the space of three or four years he travelled most of the distance from *Dubliners* to *Finnegans Wake*.

These rapid changes in Joyce's technical aims are reflected in the radical alteration of his method of composition. The late work on *Ulysses* reveals a process almost the opposite of that which transformed *Stephen Hero* into *Portrait of the Artist*. In revising *Stephen Hero* Joyce exercised a rigorous selectivity, discarding the multiple events and elaborate expository passages of the earlier work in favour of a few scenes or 'epiphanies' which embody the essential characteristics of Stephen's development. The richness of the earlier work was sacrificed in favour of intensity, and in accordance with Joyce's shifting attitude toward his own youth. But the revisions of *Ulysses* undertaken during the last years of its composition were seldom selective. They were almost entirely expansive, and the economy Joyce exercised in achieving isolated effects was overshadowed by the incessant elaborations. The ideal of dramatic compression that governed the recasting of *Stephen Hero* was replaced by an ideal of inclusiveness. In one of his early notebooks, dating from 1904, Joyce jotted down the phrase 'centripetal writing'.[54] His early revisions of *Dubliners* and the autobiographical novel *were* 'centripetal', turning in upon a few dramatic situations. But the revisions of *Ulysses* were centrifugal, moving further and further away from the conventional centres of action. Fortunately the human forces of Bloom and Stephen, and the momentum established in the early chapters, kept the revisions of *Ulysses* from completely overshadowing the *données* of each episode. But in *Finnegans Wake*, where the process of revision was intensified and carried out over a much longer period of time, one often finds crucial elements in the first drafts which have been totally obscured by the time the final version is reached.

This movement from 'centripetal' to 'centrifugal' writing during the evolution of *Ulysses* mirrors a general change in Joyce's artistic stance. A process of selectivity harmonizes with his early notion of the 'epiphany', which assumes that it is possible to reveal a whole area of experience through a single gesture or phrase. In shaping the *Portrait* Joyce sought continually to create 'epiphanies', and to define Stephen's attitudes by a stringent process of exclusion; later in his career he attempted to define by a process of inclusion. The earlier method implies that there is a significance, a 'quidditas', residing in each thing, and that the task of the artist is to discover this significance by a process of distillation. In the later method it is the artist who creates the significance through language. Thus in the *Portrait* a single gesture may reveal a character's essential nature; but in *Finnegans Wake*

Humphrey Chimpden Earwicker's nature is established by multiple relationships with all the fallen heroes of history and legend.

Succeeding chapters will examine in more detail the implications of Joyce's late work on *Ulysses*, and attempt to formulate those artistic ideals which emerged during the making of *Ulysses* and governed all of his work on *Finnegans Wake*. However, it seems appropriate at this point to seek for the reasons behind Joyce's growing interest in formal—almost mechanical—designs. What rationale can we provide for the elaborate patterns of analogy characteristic of each episode, patterns which often (as in *Oxen of the Sun*) seem grotesquely over-elaborate? To what extent is the *schema* of the novel an essential adjunct to the human drama?

First it must be acknowledged that the 'epic' proportions of *Ulysses* are absolutely dependent on the major Homeric analogues and, to a lesser extent, on the other ordering frames. But can we justify these intricate elaborations solely on this ground? I do not think so; at least two other factors must be considered.

One of these is Joyce's increasing preoccupation with linguistic experimentation, his desire to stretch the potentialities of English prose in all directions. This desire was bound up with a sheer delight in verbal manipulation, a delight which permeates these remarks to Frank Budgen concerning *Oxen of the Sun*:

Am working hard at *Oxen of the Sun*, the idea being the crime committed against fecundity by sterilizing the act of coition. Scene: Lying-in-hospital. Technique: a ninepart episode without divisions introduced by a Sallustian-Tacitean prelude (the unfertilized ovum), then by way of earliest English alliterative and monosyllabic and Anglo-Saxon ('Before born the babe had bliss. Within the womb he won worship.' 'Bloom dull dreamy heard: in held hat stony staring.') then by way of Mandeville ... then Malory's *Morte d'Arthur* ... then a passage solemn, as of Milton, Taylor, Hooker, followed by a Latin-gossipy bit, style of Burton/Browne, then a passage Bunyanesque ... After a diary-style bit Pepys-Evelyn ... and so on through Defoe-Swift and Steele-Addison-Sterne and Landor-Pater-Newman until it ends in a frightful jumble of pidgin English, nigger English, Cockney, Irish, Bowery slang and broken doggerel. This procession is also linked back at each part subtly with some foregoing episode of the day and, besides this, with the natural stages of development in the embryo and the periods of faunal evolution in general. The double-thudding Anglo-Saxon motive recurs from time to time ('Loth to move from Horne's house') to give the sense of the hoofs of oxen. Bloom is the spermatozoon, the hospital the womb, the nurse the ovum, Stephen the embryo.

How's that for High?[55]

But beyond the function of the *schema* as an essential vehicle for Joyce's themes, and as a vehicle for his restless experimentation, we must acknowledge its function as the source of 'neutral' but controlling designs. In his attempt to compose an epic of a single day, and to record the internal as well as the external lives of his characters, Joyce sacrificed many of the traditional unities of the novel. The well-made novel of the nineteenth century, founded on chronological action and composed of dramatic and expository passages (Henry James's 'drama' and 'picture'), possessed a form which Joyce could no longer employ. In 1919, while part of *Ulysses* was being serialized in the *Little Review* and the *Egoist*, Virginia Woolf defined Joyce's break with traditional forms of expression:

... he is concerned at all costs to reveal the flickerings of that innermost flame which flashes its messages through the brain, and in order to preserve it he disregards with complete courage whatever seems to him adventitious, whether it be probability, or coherence or any other of these signposts which for generations have served to support the imagination of a reader when called upon to imagine what he can neither touch nor see.[56]

Here is a clear recognition that Joyce consciously rejected those traditional 'supports' which provided order for both author and reader; but Virginia Woolf does not describe the radical innovations which replaced them. In his attempt to bring the effects of poetry to the novel, to 'internalize' the narration and record various levels of consciousness, Joyce needed as many formal orders as possible to encompass and control his work. And as conventional representation decreased in importance toward the end of *Ulysses*, the need for other patterns increased. The multiple designs Joyce wove into *Ulysses* provide a stable scaffold for the reader, but the 'support' they gave to Joyce may have been even greater. Most criticism of *Ulysses* is founded on the assumption that the essential life of the novel lies in the elaborate scheme of correspondences which Joyce revealed to his early commentators; but anyone who has examined his worksheets will realize that many of the correspondences represented for Joyce a kind of 'neutral' order. They provided frames which could control his diverse materials without merging into them. Deprived of the traditional orders of home, country and religion, Joyce had a desperate and rather untidy passion for order of any kind. All sorts of mechanical systems are used on the note-sheets to organize the diverse elements. While writing the last episode Joyce kept a sketch-map of Gibraltar before him, not because there is a complicated use of geographical detail in Molly's monologue but because the map provided Joyce with fixed points of reference. Similarly, there are many more Homeric references on the *Ulysses* note-sheets than ever made their way into the text, and we are forced to conclude that the parallel with the *Odyssey* was more useful to Joyce during the process of composition than it is to us while we read the book. Time and again he spoke of the comfort he derived from the narrative order of the *Odyssey*: it provided him—in his own words—with fixed 'ports of call'.[57] The major parallels between the wanderings of Mr. Bloom and those of Ulysses are an important dimension of the novel, but in working out the trivial details of the Homeric correspondence Joyce was exploring his own materials, not preparing clues for future readers.

We have already seen the care Joyce took during the course of composition to define the various qualities symbolized by 'Moly', the magic herb which saves Ulysses from Circe's magic. But are we as readers expected to discover and relate to each other the multiple equivalents enumerated on the note-sheets? Probably not. In this case, as in so many others, the detailed working-out of a 'correspondence' was primarily for Joyce's benefit, a part of the rigid discipline he had to undergo in order to control his disparate materials. Many of these detailed schemes lurk in the background of the novel, like the discarded scaffolding of a building which reflects its external form but tells us little of the essential nature. It would be a grave mistake to found any interpretation of *Ulysses* on Joyce's *schema*, rather than on the human actions of Stephen, and Molly, and Mr. Leopold Bloom.

NOTES FOR SECTION I

1. Georges Borach, 'Conversations with James Joyce', trans. Joseph Prescott, *College English*, XV (March 1954), 325. Borach is recalling a conversation of 1 August 1917.

2. W. B. Stanford, *The Ulysses Theme*, Oxford, 1954, pp. 186–87. Stanford was the first to discover that Joyce had to read the first seven chapters of Lamb's *Adventures of Ulysses* in 1893–94 while preparing for the Intermediate Examination in English. See his useful studies of Joyce's early contact with the *Odyssey* in *Envoy*, V (April 1951), 62–69, and *The Listener*, XLVI (19 July 1951), 99, 105. Kevin Sullivan has also examined Joyce's reading of Lamb in *Joyce among the Jesuits*, New York, 1958, pp. 94–98.

3. *Letters*, 193. JJ to Mrs. William Murray, 10 Nov. 1922.

4. Gorman, 45. At Belvedere College Joyce wrote an essay on Ulysses as 'My Favourite Hero'.

5. Gorman, 176. See also Ellmann, 238–39. The versions quoted here are based upon my reading of the original letters (now in the Cornell University Library).

6. See Richard Levin and Charles Shattuck, 'First Flight to Ithaca', in *James Joyce: Two Decades of Criticism*, ed. Seon Givens, New York, 1948, pp. 47–94. Levin and Shattuck argue for a deliberate parallel with the *Odyssey* embracing all fifteen stories, but their reasoning is forced when they reach *The Dead*. For the date of *The Dead*, see Ellmann, 252ff.

7. Ellmann, 274–75.

8. Richard Ellmann, 'The Backgrounds of *Ulysses*', *Kenyon Review*, XVI (Summer 1954), 342.

9. Gorman, 224. It is interesting to note that when Joyce began to write *Finnegans Wake*, nine years later, he also started by sketching in passages which ultimately were incorporated in the work's later episodes.

10. E. L. A., 'James Joyce to his Literary Agents', *More Books* (Boston), XVIII (Jan. 1943), 22. Letter of 22 June 1920.

11. *Letters*, 143. JJ to HSW, 12 July 1920.

12. *Letters*, 152. JJ to FB, 10 Dec. 1920.

13. Gorman, 268.

14. *Letters*, 128. JJ to HSW, 20 July 1919.

15. *Letters*, 104–05. JJ to John Quinn, 10 July 1917. Joyce began making notes for *Exiles* in Nov. 1913.

16. See Ellmann, Chap. XVII.

17. For a detailed chronology of Joyce's work on *Ulysses*, see Appendix C.

18. Gorman, 230.

19. *Letters*, 113. Ultimately the middle section contained twelve episodes.

20. *Letters*, 172. JJ to HSW, 7 Oct. 1921.

21. *Letters*, 156. JJ to John Quinn, 7 Jan. 1921.

22. *Letters*, 209–10. JJ to John Quinn, 5 Feb. 1924.

23. Slocum, 142, item E. 5. f.; from the private catalogue of Edward W. Titus, describing the set of proofs in his possession. See the entire Slocum and Cahoon description of the proofs, pp. 141–43. Some of the proofs were used by Joseph Prescott in the preparation of his unpublished doctoral thesis, 'James Joyce's *Ulysses* as a Work in Progress', Harvard University, 1944. Professor Prescott is now preparing a detailed study of Joyce's work on *Ulysses*.

24. In a letter of 22 June 1920 Joyce seems to indicate that *Circe* was the last episode to be drafted. See *Letters*, 141.

25. Frank Budgen, 'James Joyce', in *James Joyce: Two Decades of Criticism*, ed. Seon Givens, New York, 1948, p. 24.

26. Budgen, 175–77.

27. Silvio Benco, 'James Joyce in Trieste', *The Bookman* (New York), LXXII (Dec. 1930), 380.

28. The note-sheets referred to in this chapter were given to Miss Harriet Weaver in 1938 by Paul Léon, presumably at the direction of Joyce. They are now in the British Museum. For a full description of the note-sheets, see Appendix A. A more technical discussion of the notes—including the problem of their date—will be found in my article on 'Joyce's Notes for the Last Episodes of *Ulysses*', *Modern Fiction Studies*, IV (Spring 1958), 3–20.

29. *Letters*, 142.

30. Slocum, 138, item E. 5. a.

31. *Letters*, 172.

32. 'The *Ulysses* of James Joyce', *Criterion*, I (Oct. 1922), 102.

33. Budgen, 178.

34. *Letters*, 172.

35. *Letters*, 135. JJ to Frank Budgen, 3 Jan. 1920.

36. *Exiles*, ed. Padraic Colum, New York, 1951, pp. 119–20.

37. See in this connection Stuart Gilbert's *James Joyce's 'Ulysses'*, New Edn., London, 1952, pp. 85–87, where M. Bérard's theories concerning the authorship of the *Odyssey* are summarized.

38. *Literary Essays of Ezra Pound*, ed. T. S. Eliot, London, 1954, p. 406. From the 'Paris Letter' to *The Dial*, June 1922.

39. Budgen, 124–5.
40. *Letters*, 135. JJ to Mrs. William Murray, 5 Jan. 1920.
41. *Letters*, 175. JJ to Mrs. William Murray, 2 Nov. 1921.
42. Budgen, 236–37. See also *Letters*, 147–49.
43. A forthcoming study of the *Ulysses* MSS. by Professor Joseph Prescott of Wayne State University will do much to fill this need.
44. From an early fragment of the *Cyclops* episode now in the Lockwood Memorial Library, University of Buffalo (La Hune 256). The MS. dates in all probability from 1918.
45. *Little Review*, VI (Dec. 1919), 60; and VI (Jan. 1920), 53. Several obvious misprints have been silently corrected. Joyce never saw the proofs for those episodes which appeared in the *Little Review*, and the American printer occasionally deleted passages which he considered 'obscene'. The *Little Review* versions of the early episodes are substantially the same as those found in the Rosenbach MS. (see Appendix A); most of the discrepancies between the *Little Review* and the Rosenbach MS. may be accounted for by the lack of scrupulous proof-reading.
46. From a MS. version of the last half of *Nausicaa* now in the Cornell University Library, p. 32. It probably dates from early 1920.
47. Budgen, 20.
48. For other references to 'Mirus bazaar' see U 180, 251, 473, 563. The alteration from 'aid' to 'search' occurred on the proof-sheets; see Joseph Prescott, 'Stylistic Realism in Joyce's *Ulysses*', *A James Joyce Miscellany: Second Series*, ed. Marvin Magalaner, Carbondale, 1959, p. 18.
49. From Cornell *Nausicaa* MS., p. 28.
50. See *Stephen Hero*, ed. Theodore Spencer, New Edn., New York, 1955, p. 97.
51. Several versions of this *schema* are available: see Gilbert, *James Joyce's 'Ulysses'*, p. 41, and Hugh Kenner, *Dublin's Joyce*, Bloomington, 1956, pp. 226–27. The most complete reproduction of the *schema* will be found in *A James Joyce Miscellany: Second Series*, p. 48.
52. One version of this chart is now in the Cornell collection; a more detailed version, with verbal annotations, is among the *Ulysses* note-sheets in the British Museum.
53. See A. M. Klein's brilliant analysis of the episode, *Here and Now*, I (Jan. 1949), 28–48.
54. Gorman, 136.
55. *Letters*, 138–39. JJ to Frank Budgen, 13 March 1920.
56. Virginia Woolf, 'Modern Fiction', *The Common Reader: First and Second Series*, New York, 1948, p. 214.
57. *Letters*, 204.

CONVERSION TABLE FOR *ULYSSES*

The right-hand column gives a rough indication of the number of pages that must be subtracted from references to the Modern Library (Random

House) *Ulysses* in order to obtain page references for the 1937 English edition (John Lane, the Bodley Head).

Modern Library	Bodley Head
5	− 4
50	− 4
100	− 6
150	− 9
200	− 9
250	− 9
300	− 10
350	− 10
400	− 11
450	− 13
500	− 15
550	− 17
600	− 22
650	− 23
700	− 24
750	− 26

II

NEW BEARINGS

1. EXPRESSIVE FORM

> My intention is to transpose the myth *sub specie temporis nostri*.
> Each adventure (that is, every hour, every organ, every art being
> interconnected and interrelated in the structural scheme of the
> whole) should not only condition but even create its own
> technique.   Joyce in 1920[1]

IN *The Sacred River* L. A. G. Strong tells of a revealing conversation between Joyce and Frank O'Connor. The scene is Joyce's flat: O'Connor has just touched the frame of a picture on the wall.

'What's this?'
'Cork'.
'Yes, I see it's Cork. I was born there. But what's the frame?'
'Cork'.[2]

This anecdote illuminates one of Joyce's major artistic techniques, a method which increased in importance during the making of *Ulysses* until it finally dominated the late revisions. The technique—to which I have given the name 'expressive form'[3]—seeks to establish a direct correspondence between substance and style. The form 'expresses' or imitates qualities of its subject. Following this ideal, Joyce tried to endow each episode of *Ulysses* with a form which would suggest characteristics of the setting or action. Thus an episode which takes place in a newspaper office is cast in the form of a newspaper, or a section on sentimental girlhood is written in a 'namby-pamby jammy marmalady drawersy (alto là!) style'.[4] Since all art is 'expressive' to some degree, we can define Joyce's extreme use of the technique by observing that late in the writing of *Ulysses* he had reached a point where he was willing to imitate in the novel's

44

form the irrational, chaotic or trivial qualities of its subject-matter. This attempt to give the technique a maximum freedom was directly responsible for the failure of the *Eumaeus* episode, where Joyce succeeded in 'expressing' the fatigue of Bloom and Stephen. One is reminded of Scott's remark that Jane Austen ran the risk of boring her readers by a faithful rendering of dull characters; or of the partial failure that occurs near the end of the *Waste Land*, when Eliot seeks to mirror the theme of fragmentation in the poem's form. There is a vast difference between Gerty MacDowell's schoolgirl language in *Nausicaa*, which is circumscribed and controlled by the larger form of the episode, and the relinquishment to fatigue in *Eumaeus*. But with his 'expressive' techniques, as with all others, Joyce was not content until he had exploited their possibilities to the fullest; they contribute to most of the successes as well as the failures of *Finnegans Wake*. In one sense the method is a substitute for the old notion of 'levels of style', except in this case every element of existence is given its appropriate and unique form.

An examination of the notes Joyce kept before him late in the writing of *Ulysses* reveals his preoccupation with 'expressive' devices. The 'expressive form' of the *Ithaca* episode, where 'all events are resolved into their cosmic, physical, psychical etc. equivalents',[5] is reflected on the note-sheets by a multitude of mathematical calculations and facts from the natural sciences, many of which do not appear in the published version. These unused notations were dissipated in the course of composition; they were part of a preparatory process necessary to Joyce but largely irrelevant to an understanding of the novel. The *Ithaca* notes are couched in mathematical jargon, so that the mystery of the Trinity becomes, in an unused entry, $JC = \sqrt[3]{God}$. In carrying the harmony of matter and style to this extreme, Joyce was 'working himself into' the expressive form of the episode.

On one of the note-sheets for the last episode, *Penelope*, we find the entry 'gynomorphic', a reminder that the form of the episode is shaped by the physical characteristics of the female sex. In a letter to Frank Budgen Joyce spoke of his 'expressive' intent in *Penelope*:

It [Molly's monologue] begins and ends with the female word *Yes*. It turns like the huge earthball slowly surely and evenly round and round spinning. Its four cardinal points being the female breasts, arse, womb and ... [sic] expressed by the words *because, bottom* (in all senses, bottom button, bottom of the glass, bottom of the sea, bottom of his heart) *woman, yes*.[6]

Molly is the Earth, Gea-Tellus, the fixed point that determines the orbits of Bloom and Stephen, who are compared with comets in the *Ithaca* episode. Evidence that Joyce kept this correspondence and the 'expressive' words of Molly's monologue constantly before him may be found in the following notes, from a sheet containing words and phrases for the closing pages of the novel.

MB = spinning Earth
yes, yes, yes, yes, yes.

A measure of Joyce's preoccupation with 'expressive form' during the last stages of his work on *Ulysses* may be obtained by comparing those versions of the early episodes which appeared in the *Little Review* of 1918 with the final text. As test cases I have chosen two chapters which underwent extensive revision, the *Lotus-eaters* (which was first published in July 1918) and *Aeolus* (October 1918).[7]

During the revisions of 1920–21 the form of the *Lotus-eaters* episode was radically altered. In November of 1920 Joyce wrote to John Quinn: 'The episodes which have the heaviest burden of addenda are *Lotus-eaters*, *Lestrygonians*, *Nausikaa* and *Cyclops*.'[8] And almost a year later, in a letter to Harriet Weaver, he described the episode as 'much amplified' in its final version.[9] In this episode Mr. Bloom enters the post office, where he collects a letter from Martha; reads the letter; visits All Hallows church; stops at the chemist's; and finally heads toward the 'mosque of the baths' (U 85). These events suggest the episode's 'scheme': if we follow Joyce's chart the dominant Organs are the genitals; the Art, chemistry; the Symbol, the Eucharist; and the Technic, narcissism. Furthermore, the Homeric analogue and the oriental motif suggest flower images: Bloom's pseudonym in his correspondence with Martha is 'Henry Flower', and the names of many flowers are woven into the text, just as five years later Joyce was to weave hundreds of river-names into the *Anna Livia Plurabelle* section of *Finnegans Wake*.

Many of Joyce's late additions to the *Lotus-eaters* simply strengthen the episode's *leitmotifs*, as in the following allusions to the bath and baptism which are not found in the *Little Review*:

He stood a moment unseeing by the cold black marble bowl while before him and behind two worshippers dipped furtive hands in the low tide of holy water (U 82).

However, most of Joyce's alterations and amplifications were designed to 'express' the nature of the episode, as in these passages where the changes are aimed at creating that 'language of flowers' to which Bloom makes a passing reference. I have italicized the relevant addenda.

Lovely spot it must be: the garden of the world, big lazy leaves, shaky lianas they call them. Wonder is it like that. Those Cinghalese lobbing around in the sun, not doing a damn tap all day. Influence of the climate. Where was the chap I saw in that picture somewhere?[10]

Lovely spot it must be: the garden of the world, big lazy leaves to float about on, *cactuses, flowery meads,* snaky lianas they call them. Wonder is it like that. Those Cinghalese lobbing around in the sun, in *dolce far niente*. Not doing a hand's turn all day. Sleep six months out of twelve. Too hot to quarrel. Influence of the climate. Lethargy. *Flowers of idleness. The air feeds most. Azotes. Hothouse in Botanic gardens. Sensitive plants. Waterlilies. Petals too tired to.* Sleeping sickness in the air. *Walk on roseleaves.* Imagine trying to eat tripe and cowheel. Where was the chap I saw in that picture somewhere? (U 70–71).

He tore the flower gravely from its pinhold and placed it in his heart pocket. Then, walking slowly forward, he read the letter again, murmuring here and there a word. Having read it all he took it from the newspaper and put it back in his sidepocket.[11]

He tore the flower gravely from its pinhold smelt its almost no smell and placed it in his heart pocket. *Language of flowers. They like it because no-one can hear. Or a poison bouquet to strike him down.* Then, walking slowly forward, he read the letter again, murmuring here and there a word. *Angry tulips with you darling manflower punish your cactus if you don't please poor forgetmenot how I long violets to dear roses when we soon anemone meet all naughty nightstalk wife Martha's perfume.* Having read it all he took it from the newspaper and put it back in his sidepocket (U 77).

The manner in which Joyce established the episode's various correspondences and re-shaped the prose to 'express' the nature of Bloom's experiences is beautifully illustrated by his revision of the final passage, which read as follows in 1918:

Enjoy a bath now: clean trough of water, cool enamel, the gentle tepid stream. He foresaw his pale body reclined in it at full, naked, oiled by scented melting soap, softly laved. He saw his trunk and limbs riprippled over and sustained, buoyed lightly upward, lemonyellow: saw the dark tangled curls of his bush floating, floating hair of the stream around a languid floating flower.[12]

The expansions of 1920–21 produced this final version: I have italicized the addenda.

Enjoy a bath now: clean trough of water, cool enamel, the gentle tepid stream. *This is my body.*

He foresaw his pale body reclined in it at full, naked, *in a womb of warmth,* oiled by scented melting soap, softly laved. He saw his trunk and limbs riprippled over and sustained, buoyed lightly upward, lemonyellow: *his navel, bud of flesh:* and saw the dark tangled curls of his bush floating, floating hair of the stream around *the limp father of thousands,* a languid floating flower (U 85).

Here the revisions, typical of Joyce's elaborative method, were designed to express the complex correspondences of *Lotus-eaters*. The insertion of 'This is my body' emphasizes the motif of the Eucharist; 'womb of warmth' reinforces the theme of narcissism; and the other additions connect the organ of the episode and the oriental motif with the 'language of flowers'.

'*Eolus* is recast', Joyce wrote to Harriet Weaver in October 1921.[13] Of all the episodes which appeared in the *Little Review*, the *Aeolus* chapter was subjected to the most significant revisions. The recasting of the episode followed a characteristic pattern of expansion and elaboration. Scarcely a word of the original text was changed; instead, Joyce inserted phrases, sentences and whole paragraphs in his drive toward a more 'expressive' form.

The episode takes place in a newspaper office, and the Homeric parallel is Ulysses' disastrous adventure at the isle of Aeolus, identified by modern commentators with the volcano Stromboli.[14] Consequently it is appropriate that the Organ celebrated should be the lungs; the Art, rhetoric; and the Colour, red. The episode is filled with allusions to wind and the human voice, while its language is consciously rhetorical (Stuart Gilbert lists over ninety different rhetorical devices used in the episode).[15] The text is divided into sections with captions that imitate newspaper headlines; viewed as a sequence, these captions reflect the historical development of journalistic style.

All these correspondences and parallels, familiar to a reader of the final version, were almost non-existent in the 1918 form. In the *Little Review* the episode appeared as an unbroken narrative, without the newspaper headlines; a late addition, they exhibit Joyce's unceasing effort to duplicate the form of his subject-matter in the form of his expression.

Another change indicative of Joyce's aesthetic aims was the increase in different rhetorical forms. Of the ninety-five devices listed by Gilbert, thirty were the result of Joyce's late revisions, and these thirty provide the margin that makes rhetorical experimentation such an obvious chractertistic of *Aeolus*. For instance, in revising a single page three new figures were added to Lenehan's conversation, primarily for the purpose of enriching Joyce's catalogue:

—Madam, I'm Adam. And Able was I ere I saw Elba. (*Palindrome*)
—The father of scare journalism ... and the brother-in-law of Chris Callinan. (*Zeugma*)
—Clamn dever ... (*Metathesis*)

(U 135–36)

Or compare the first sentence of the *Little Review* version with the revised form:

Grossbooted draymen rolled barrels dullthudding out of Prince's stores and bumped them up on the brewery float. Grossbooted draymen rolled barrels dullthudding out of Prince's stores and bumped them up on the brewery float.[16]

*   *   *   *

Grossbooted draymen rolled barrels dullthudding out of Prince's stores and bumped them up on the brewery float. On the brewery float bumped dullthudding barrels rolled by grossbooted draymen out of Prince's stores (U 115).

Here, by reversing the word order in the second sentence, Joyce has added another figure (*Chiasmus*) to his scheme. In the same manner, he sought to emphasize the episode's dominant colour (red) by a series of minor alterations; for example, Murray's first name is changed from 'John' to 'Red', and J. J. O'Molloy acquires a 'hectic flush' (U 124).

The winds of fatuous journalism and inflated rhetoric, along with Stromboli's hot fumes and the Aeolian winds, blow through the episode. In the final stages of revision the style was re-worked to express this 'windiness'. The late additions are packed with references to wind and the human voice: 'wind' (U 116), '*fanned by gentlest zephyrs'* (122), 'Windfall', 'gale days' (123), 'What's in the wind' (124), 'O, HARP EOLIAN' (126), 'There's a hurricane blowing' (127), 'blowing' (128), 'vent' (129), 'O, for a fresh of breath air!' (133), 'Windy Arbour', 'breath of life' (135), 'blown down by that cyclone' (136), 'divine afflatus' (138), 'four winds', 'voice', 'You take my breath away', 'windy Troy' (142), 'breathless', 'puffing' (144), 'squalls', and 'raise the wind' (145). As with the rhetorical figures, Joyce tried to give these reminders of his *schema* unobtrusive positions in the narrative, but he did not always succeed. Any one of the five references to wind introduced by Joyce in his revision of the following passage is appropriate to Bloom's normal speech, but taken together they seem a little forced.

Practice dwindling. Losing heart. Used to get good retainers from D. and T. Fitzgerald. Believe he does some literary work for the *Express* with Gabriel Conroy. Well-read fellow. Myles Crawford began on the *Independent*. Funny the way they veer about. Go for one another baldheaded in the papers and then hail fellow well met the next moment.[17]

Practice dwindling. A might-havebeen. Losing heart. Gambling. Debts of honour. Reaping the *whirlwind*. Used to get good retainers from D. and T. Fitzgerald. Their wigs to show their grey matter. Brains on their sleeve like the statue in Glasnevin. Believe he does some literary work for the *Express* with Gabriel Conroy. Wellread fellow. Myles Crawford began on the *Independent*. Funny the way those newspaper men veer about when they get *wind* of a new opening. *Weathercocks*. Hot and cold in the same *breath*. Wouldn't know which to believe. One story good till you hear the next. Go for one another baldheaded in the papers and then all *blows* over. Hailfellow well met the next moment (U 124; italics mine).

An appreciation of Joyce's 'expressive' aims helps us to understand his late work on *Ulysses*, and demonstrates the extent to which he was preoccupied with the novel's *schema* at that stage in the process of composition. It also prepares us for one of the most obvious techniques of *Finnegans Wake*. The revisions examined in this chapter reflect a movement toward what Kenneth Burke has called 'onomatopoetic correspondence between form and theme',[18] and in the *Wake* 'onomatopoetic correspondence' lies at the heart of Joyce's method.

This increasing emphasis on 'expressive form' may also be seen as one explanation for Joyce's shift to expansive revision. The artistic effects he sought to achieve while reworking the early episodes and writing the later ones do not depend on our conscious recognition of the analogies he was strengthening. As readers we do not catalogue the references to flowers, nor count the rhetorical figures; but we do feel the accumulative force of their repetition. And such accumulative effects could only be produced by a process of elaboration.

It should be obvious from the passages cited in this chapter that Joyce, in revising *Ulysses*, ran the danger of placing disproportionate emphasis on the *schema* of the novel. The analogy between Bloom's adventures in the newspaper office and Ulysses' at the isle of Aeolus is a secondary aspect of the episode, and the various correspondences (Colour, Art, Organ) are less important than the dissection of Irish public life or the development of Bloom's character. However, Joyce's revisions placed these secondary qualities in a prominent position, and although they do not obscure the episode's major themes there is a significant shift in emphasis between the 1918 and 1922 versions. The *schema* upon which Joyce relied during his revisions was overemphasized. We shall see later that in the revisions of *Finnegans Wake*, where Joyce employed more radical techniques over a longer period of time, the 'expressive' intent often smothered important elements which were quite clear in the early drafts.

2. THE 'IMAGE'

An 'Image' is that which presents an intellectual and emotional complex in an instant of time. . . .

It is the presentation of such a 'complex' instantaneously which gives that sense of sudden liberation; that sense of freedom from time limits and space limits; that sense of sudden growth, which we experience in the presence of the greatest works of art.

Ezra Pound in 1913[19]

A revolution in sensibility demands new techniques. When traditional ways of knowing the world collapse traditional forms of expression are invalidated. In desperation the artist turns to new areas of experience in search of vitality and authority: Pound's orientalism, Yeats's esoteric mysticism and Joyce's ransacking of obscure mythologies are examples of this search. Even Eliot, while retaining the structure of Christian thought, incorporated the discoveries of modern anthropology and psychology into his poetry. In the second and third decades of this century our greatest artists found the inherited forms of communication unsuited to their new visions, and began to experiment with more radical techniques. At the centre of this experimentation lay the doctrine of the 'Image', an aesthetic concept which illuminates Joyce's mature methods.

The 'Imagist' movement in modern poetry, first announced to the public in 1913 by Ezra Pound, produced a limited amount of distinguished verse; its most important achievement was the formulation of certain aesthetic principles which were shared by a large number of contemporary writers and which were of far-reaching significance in the development of modern literature.[20] Although Joyce was never a part of the movement, his early experiments in technique and his wide reading of Continental literature had led him to many of the conclusions articulated by Pound. The poems of *Chamber Music* (1907) exhibit 'Imagist' qualities, as Pound acknowledged when he published Poem XXXVI ('I hear an army') in the *Des Imagistes* anthology. These affinities justify our use of the Imagist position as a starting point in examining one phase of Joyce's technique.

In Ernest Fenollosa's essay on *The Chinese Written Character as a Medium for Poetry* Pound found support for his doctrine of the 'Image'.[21] Fenollosa's emphasis is two-fold: he contrasts the concreteness of the Chinese character with the abstract nature of Western discourse, and compares its immediacy with the discursive arguments of Western prose. Pound summarizes these distinctions in his *ABC of Reading*:

In Europe, if you ask a man to define anything, his definition always moves away from the simple things that he knows perfectly well, it recedes into an unknown region, that is a region of remoter and progressively remoter abstraction.

Thus if you ask him what red is, he says it is a 'colour'.

If you ask him what a colour is, he tells you it is a vibration or a refraction of light, or a division of the spectrum.

And if you ask him what vibration is, he tells you it is a mode of energy, or something of that sort, until you arrive at a modality of being, or non-being, or at any rate you get in beyond your depth, and beyond his depth.[22]

But, says Pound, the Chinese employ a radically different method and communicate the concept 'red' by juxtaposing the abbreviated pictures of four familiar sense-objects: rose, iron rust, cherry and flamingo.[23] Thus the concept is defined concretely, and the 'complex' is apprehended—in theory at least—'in an instant of time'. The dimension of the Chinese character is spatial rather than temporal: it is an 'Image'.

The essence of the 'Image', as Pound describes its operation, is *simultaneity* of effect. We usually think of such simultaneity as the property of the visual arts, since in music and literature the necessary flow of form through time (one chord after another, one word after another) complicates the presentation of 'an intellectual and emotional complex in an instant of time'. But it is obvious that even in the visual arts our apprehension of an 'Image' is the result of an accumulative process: *simultaneity* can only be obtained after we are familiar with all the components and their relationships with each other. This process of gradual apprehension is discussed by Stephen in *Portrait of the Artist*:

An aesthetic image is presented to us either in space or in time. What is audible is presented in time, what is visible is presented in space. But temporal or spatial, the aesthetic image is first luminously apprehended as selfbounded and selfcontained upon the immeasurable background of space or time which is not it. . . . You apprehend its wholeness. That is *integritas*.[24]

Stephen goes on to say that after apprehending the 'wholeness' of the 'aesthetic image' one proceeds to an apprehension of the harmonious 'rhythm of its structure', and finally to a recognition of its 'scholastic *quidditas*', its exact spiritual equivalent.[25] Although Stephen's aesthetic must not be identified with that of the mature Joyce, there seems no reason to question the general validity of this argument. Total apprehension of any complex artistic structure is the culmination of a process, and that process exists in time.

The emphasis on instantaneous perception which is central to Pound's theory manifests itself in his 'Imagist' verse. A short poem such as 'Papyrus' is designed to present 'an intellectual and emotional complex in an instant of time.'

> Spring . . . . .
> Too long . . . .
> Gongula . . . .[26]

Here, from two fragments of a text and the signature of a young girl, one pieces together a poignant love-letter. Pound suggests, the reader must reconstruct. The process of apprehension is almost instantaneous, but there are still discernible stages in our progress toward total awareness. The linear movement of language, which is similar to the melodic line in music, prevents an instantaneous 'pictorial' grasping of the poem. Joyce's work on

Ulysses and *Finnegans Wake* is characterized by a growing conflict between his aesthetic ideal of 'simultaneity' and the consecutive nature of language.

As *Ulysses* and *Finnegans Wake* developed Joyce moved further and further from the conventions of sequence and order established by traditional fiction. Because of its relevance to his method, Joyce took particular delight in Hamlet's remark to Rosencrantz and Guildenstern:

O God! I could be bounded in a nutshell, and count myself a king of infinite space; were it not that I have bad dreams. (II. ii. 257–59)

Hamlet's lament becomes, in the distorted idiom of *Finnegans Wake*, 'Putting Allspace in a Notshall' (455/29). In pursuit of his goal of putting Allspace (and consequently all Time) in the nutshell world of his art, Joyce abandoned consecutive narration in favour of a 'pictorial' or spatial method. Frank Budgen, who knew Joyce's mind as well as anyone, recognized the painter's sensibility:

Joyce may be musical in taste rather than pictorial, yet his view of life is that of a painter surveying a still scene rather than that of a musician following a development through time.[27]

In writing *Ulysses* Joyce retained on one level the chronological order of conventional fiction: the immediate experiences of the characters are described in the order of their occurrence. But only the events of 16 June 1904 are given this chronological order. All the elements provided by memory or association come to the reader piecemeal, and cannot be fully understood until the novel has been read many times. In a sense, as Joseph Frank says, 'Joyce cannot be read—he can only be re-read.'

A knowledge of the whole is essential to an understanding of any part; but unless one is a Dubliner, such knowledge can be obtained only after the book has been read and all the references fitted into their proper place and grasped as a unity. Although the burdens placed on the reader by this method of composition may seem insuperable, the fact remains that Joyce, in his unbelievably laborious fragmentation of narrative structure, proceeded on the assumption that a unified spatial apprehension of his work would ultimately be possible.[28]

Once the events and themes of *Ulysses* have become familiar, the entire work stands before one as a vast static 'Image'. And when the book is re-read with this 'complex' in mind, each succeeding passage yields a new set of relationships. Of course, the demands upon memory and imagination are prodigious; but they are prodigiously rewarding. The reader recreates in his mind an approximation of that total design which guided Joyce in the process of composition.

Unlike *Ulysses*, *Finnegans Wake* is based upon a stylized 'dream-logic', and there is no obvious narrative level to draw the reader's interest and establish a fundamental line of development. There is really no development at all, in the conventional sense, for the book's cyclic structure eliminates 'beginning, middle and end'. Edmund Wilson has mentioned as a 'serious defect' the fact 'that we do not really understand what is happening till we have almost finished the book'.[29] I would emend this to read 'till we have finished the book several times'. One cannot fully comprehend the basic themes of the opening episodes until after an exhaustive study of the entire work; each passage depends as much upon what follows as upon what precedes it. At first one reads the *Wake* for its humour and Joyce's linguistic virtuosity, for the frequently moving passages and sudden illuminations; systematic understanding comes later and with much re-reading.

The demands upon the reader's memory and imagination made by *Ulysses* and *Finnegans Wake* are not unique with Joyce, although they exceed those made by any other modern novelist. In the novels of Virginia Woolf and William Faulkner there is the same tendency toward 'Imagist' structure. In *The Sound and the Fury*, for example, the events are first presented with no regard for their actual chronology, through the associational reverie of the idiot Benjy. Then they are rehearsed from two biased points-of-view in the narratives of Quentin and Jason. Finally, in the fourth section, Faulkner himself provides the missing information and necessary perspective. The first section cannot be fully understood until the last has been read, and after the reader has finished the novel he must reorganize the novel's narrative fragments into a single pattern. The same technique is used by Proust, who depends on the imagination of the reader to fuse the 'moments' of his great work 'reflexively in a moment of time.'[30]

The 'Imagist' nature of *Ulysses* and *Finnegans Wake* could be deduced from Joyce's methods of composition. As we have seen, the total design of *Ulysses* was before Joyce during most of his work on the novel, and he could turn to first one, then another part of his 'mosaic', elaborating upon the basic pattern. In a later chapter I shall demonstrate that Joyce was in command of the final structure of *Finnegans Wake* at an early date. In the case of both works he spent most of his time embroidering upon a static pattern. Edmund Wilson has an interesting comment on this aspect of Joyce's method:

His force, instead of following a line, expands itself in every dimension (including that of Time) about a single point. The world of 'Ulysses' is animated by a complex inexhaustible life: we revisit it as we do a city, where we come more and more to recognize faces, to understand personalities, to grasp relations, currents and interests. Joyce has exercised considerable technical ingenuity in introducing us to the elements of his story in an order which will enable us to find our bearings: yet I doubt whether any human memory is capable, on a first reading, of meeting the demands of 'Ulysses'. And when we reread it, we start in at any point, as if it were indeed something solid like a city which actually existed in space and which could be entered from any direction—as Joyce is said, in composing his books, to work on the different parts simultaneously.[31]

One problem that confronted Joyce in his pursuit of simultaneity has already been mentioned. What Frank calls the 'inherent consecutiveness of language'[32] prevents that immediate perception of 'an intellectual and emotional complex' which Pound desired: unity is only achieved in retrospect or after extensive re-reading. Pound's *Cantos*, in their disregard for conventions of sequence and transition, are open to attack on this ground. But Joyce is even more vulnerable, for whereas Pound tried to 'get down all the colours or elements' of his poem in the opening cantos,[33] Joyce abandoned even this vestige of narrative form in making *Finnegans Wake*. Pound, in accordance with his 'Ideogrammic' method, relied primarily on juxtaposition and association to obtain his effects, yet he did retain the consecutive logic of language. But Joyce sought in *Finnegans Wake* to transform each word into a miniature 'Image', a multiple unit capable of sounding a number of themes simultaneously.

Before proceeding with this argument we need a text for reference. Here is a passage from *Finnegans Wake* which illustrates Joyce's success in compressing a number of related themes into a single 'portmanteau' unit.

So hath been, love: tis tis: and will be: till wears and tears and ages. Thief us the night, steal we the air, shawl thiner liefest, mine! Here, Ohere, insult the fair! Traitor, bad hearer, brave! The lightning look, the birding cry, awe from the grave, everflowing on the times. Feueragusaria iordenwater; now godsun shine on menday's daughter; a good clap, a fore marriage, a bad wake, tell hell's well; such is manowife's lot of lose and win again, like he's gruen quhiskers on who's chin again, she plucketed them out but they grown in again. So what are you going to do about it? O dear!

If juness she saved! Ah ho! And if yulone he pouved! The olold stoliolum! From quiqui quinet to michemiche chelet and a jambe-batiste to a brulobrulo! . . . this oldworld epistola of their weatherings and their marryings and their buryings and their natural selections . . . (FW 116/36–117/28)

The four-part statements which make up most of this passage are grouped together because of their common relationship to the

Viconian cycles which govern the *Wake*. This relationship is so exact—almost mechanical—that it can best be presented in schematic form.

VICONIAN PERIOD	DIVINE	HEROIC	CIVIL	RICORSO
INSTITUTION	RELIGION	MARRIAGE	BURIAL	
INDIVIDUAL SIGNIFICANCE	BIRTH	MARRIAGE	DEATH	RESURRECTION
So hath been, love:	tis tis:	and will be:	till wears and tears and ages.
Thief us the night,	steal we the air,	shawl thiner liefest,	mine!
The lightning look,	the bird- ing cry,	awe from the grave,	everflowing on the times.
a good clap,	a fore marriage,	a bad wake,	tell hell's well;
From quiqui quinet	to michemiche chelet	and a jambebatiste	to a brulo- brulo!
their weatherings	and their marryings	and their buryings	and their natural selections

The most complex and cunning of these four-part sentences bears closer examination, since it recapitulates Vico's cycle on two levels (historical and individual) and *simultaneously* names the chief sources of Joyce's cyclic theory.

From quiqui quinet to michemiche chelet and a jambebatiste to a brulobrulo!

'Quiqui' represents the first of Vico's ages, the obscure origin of language in primitive man's first questions ('Who? What?') when faced with natural mysteries. But it also suggests human infancy, the questioning child; the individual reflects in his growth the cyclic development of the race. The connection with childhood is strengthened by the next word, 'quinet'; for Edgar Quinet, the nineteenth-century French historian, was the author of the passage in French quoted on page 281 of the *Wake*. It is evident from Joyce's re-fashioning of the passage earlier in the *Wake*, and from a letter he wrote to Harriet Weaver, that he associated the wild flowers in the quotation from Quinet with the 'lilts of children.'[34]

'Miche' means 'to pilfer' or 'to skulk'; it is also French for a round loaf of bread, and in French slang means 'bottom'. 'Pilfer' and 'skulk' suggest the Fall, the forbidden fruit and Adam and Eve hiding from the Lord. 'Skulk' also implies the guilt obsessions of adult life, which destroy the innocence of childhood and mirror the Original Fall. 'Miche' as a loaf of bread suggests the practical, breadwinning aspects of adult life, while its vulgar connotation is applicable to the Fall of Adam or Everyman's fall. Furthermore, 'michemiche' is reminiscent of 'mishe mishe' ('I am I am') on the first page of the *Wake*; and this connection illuminates the entire passage.

Compared with the multiple meanings of 'michemiche', 'jambebatiste' is relatively simple; the complex activities of adult life all come to one end. 'Jambe' and 'batiste' present an image of legs covered by cloth—the shrouded body at the wake. With equal finality, 'brulobrulo' is the Hell (Fr. *brûler*) which must precede resurrection. Taken together, the two compound words represent the death and rebirth of every man and every civilization.

Besides outlining the four-part Viconian cycle in its historical and individual phases, this sentence retraces the history of the particular world-view it expresses. 'Quinet' is Edgar Quinet, the translator of Herder and student of Vico; 'michemiche chelet' is Jules Michelet, another nineteenth-century French historian, author of the *Histoire de France* and translator of Vico; 'jambebatiste' gives us Vico's first name, Giambattista; and 'brulobrulo' is Bruno of Nola, 'burnt Bruno'. Thus each 'portmanteau' word in the sentence 'presents an intellectual and emotional complex in an instant of time.' However, this effect of simultaneity can only be appreciated by the reader after laborious exegesis.

One more important point can be deduced from the structure of this sentence and its position in the *Wake*. Just as each fragment of a mosaic is grouped with units of a similar colour and texture, so this sentence is embedded in a cluster of related Viconian allusions. But its exact position in the passage is not inevitable, and it could be exchanged with one of the other four-part statements without destroying the unity of the passage. Indeed, it could be deleted without seriously impairing the total context, and such is its relevance to the major structure of the book that it could be incorporated into any passage concerning the Viconian cycles. Language having lost its 'consecutive qualities', the unit is no longer kept in place by the strict logic of narrative movement. Instead, it is grouped with a number of similar units, and each passage is developed by a process of elaboration or accretion which has no inherent limits. As Joyce's art developed and the force of narrative logic diminished, the process of accumulative revision was intensified. In theory, any section of *Finnegans Wake* is susceptible to infinite expansion; indeed, the entire work is a prolonged expansion of a few basic concepts. In reading it one does not feel that sense of 'inevitability' or 'rightness' which is the sign of a controlled narrative structure.

3. THE CONDITION OF MUSIC

Le vers par flèches jeté moins avec succession que presque simultanément pour l'idée, réduit la durée à une division spirituelle propre au sujet: diffère de la phrase ou développement temporaire, dont la prose joue, le dissimulant, selon mille tours.

Mallarmé, 'La Musique et les lettres'[35]

It is a critical commonplace to say that Joyce's later work reflects a growing concern with the possibility of accommodating musical

and literary forms. His own love for music and understanding of
musical techniques are well-known, and all his work from
Chamber Music to *Finnegans Wake* testifies to the auditory nature
of his imagination. The near-blindness which darkened his later
years merely intensified the musical qualities which are evident
throughout his early writings. The imagery of the last poem from
Chamber Music shows how the visual effects of Joyce's youthful
work are dependent upon the auditory imagination.

> I hear an army charging upon the land,
> And the thunder of horses plunging, foam about their knees:
> Arrogant, in black armour, behind them stand,
> Disdaining the reins, with fluttering whips, the charioteers.
>
> They cry unto the night their battle-name:
> I moan in sleep when I hear afar their whirling laughter.
> They cleave the gloom of dreams, a blinding flame,
> Clanging, clanging upon the heart as upon an anvil.
>
> They come shaking in triumph their long green hair:
> They come out of the sea and run shouting by the shore.
> My heart, have you no wisdom thus to despair?
> My love, my love, my love, why have you left me alone?

Here each of the first two stanzas opens with an appeal to the
ear: then, as the stanza progresses, the image struggles into sight.
Although the total impression conveyed by the poem is strongly
pictorial—Pound chose it as an example of 'Imagist' verse—the
basic impulse springs from the auditory imagination.

In *Ulysses* the communication of setting through sound is
intensified. There is very little conventional description, the novel
is composed mainly of conversation and interior monologues; yet
when we reach the end of *Ulysses* we know Dublin in visual
terms. By his ingenious use of techniques which are primarily
aural Joyce has made the City a concrete reality to all the senses.
Stephen Dedalus suggests the secret of this method in the opening

pages of *Proteus*, where he broods on the interrelation of temporal and spatial sequences, the *nacheinander* and the *nebeneinander*: 'Shut your eyes and see' (U 38).

Joyce describes the televising of a steeplechase in *Finnegans Wake* as '*an admirable verbivocovisual presentment*' (341/18–19), and the description may be applied with justice to the entire work. In the *Wake* sight and sound merge with each other, and Joyce's polysemantic units often create memorable visual images by means of rhythm and suggestion. 'Hush! Caution! Echoland!' the reader is warned early in the *Wake*: ' 'Tis optophone which ontophanes' (13/5, 16). The optophone is a machine used by the blind which translates printed type into the medium of sound, giving the visual pattern an audible form. 'Ontophanes' is Joyce's own coinage, meaning roughly the 'showing forth' of 'being'. The entire sentence, ' 'Tis optophone which ontophanes', is a revealing statement of Joyce's aesthetic intent. It may be paraphrased as: 'Reality is presented in *Finnegans Wake* by sound patterns which communicate visual images.'

Joyce's attempt to capture for literature the advantages of musical expression is intimately connected with the movement toward 'simultaneous' presentation discussed in the preceding chapter. *Ulysses* belongs to many different traditions, one of which is the tradition of the Wagnerian novel, another that of the Symbolist poets who tried to fuse musical and poetic effects.[36] Among Joyce's precursors were all those nineteenth-century writers who strove toward Pater's 'condition of music', hoping to find a successful compromise between literary and musical forms. Almost every critic of *Ulysses* has, at one time or another, resorted to an analogy with music to clarify the structural intricacies of the novel, and although these analogies are rarely the same ('sonata', 'fugue', 'symphony', 'Wagnerian opera') they all testify to an important dimension of the work.

Ulysses makes use of those musical devices which are most 'literary', and which can be adapted to prose without radically altering its structure. Among these are 'counterpoint' and the *leitmotif*. In using these techniques Joyce was following the example of other writers before him, such as Flaubert, Dujardin, and the Symbolist poets, but he surpassed them in his determination to exploit the musical possibilities of language. *Ulysses* contains hundreds of *leitmotifs*, ranging from important associations to distinctive phrases, and these are repeated, amplified, and transformed to create a feeling of 'musical' development. Joyce delights in a contrapuntal arrangement of themes: like Proust, he relies on repetition and counterpoint to advance his work. He also makes full use of onomatopoeia to create 'tonalities'. *Ulysses*, which destroys the conventional distinctions between poetry and prose, is the fullest illustration of T. S. Eliot's assertion that poetic language can achieve many of the effects we normally associate with music:

> The use of recurrent themes is as natural to poetry as to music. There are possibilities for verse which bear some analogy to the development of a theme by different groups of instruments; there are possibilities of transitions in a poem comparable to the different movements of a symphony or a quartet; there are possibilities of contrapuntal arrangement of subject-matter.[37]

It should be noted that Eliot does not claim an exact correspondence between the techniques of literature and music; he does not call for a re-fashioning of language. Rather he claims that within the limits of linear progression the writer can create forms which 'bear some analogy to' the forms of music.

The consecutive nature of language would seem to preclude some of the simultaneous effects produced in music by orchestration or the chord, but the freedom from rigid time-limits provided by the stream-of-consciousness method and the fragmented chronological scheme enabled Joyce to explore many possibilities of musical form while writing *Ulysses*. Of all the episodes the *Sirens* is most self-consciously musical, and it demonstrates the nature and extent of those musical effects which can be achieved without destroying the rudimentary conventions of language. We may use the *Sirens* as one measure of Joyce's achievement in *Ulysses*, and as a basis for judging the radical techniques of *Finnegans Wake*.

Joyce attempted to give *Sirens* a 'fugal' form (the *schema* lists its technique as '*fuga per canonem*'), and the episode displays literary equivalents of polyphony and counterpoint. It opens with an 'overture', a catalogue of words and phrases which provides a suggestive outline of the narrative it precedes. Stuart Gilbert calls these abbreviated entries 'extracts from the narrative which follows':[38] but to view them as 'extracts' oversimplifies their intended function. All of the entries do suggest, in one way or another, subsequent passages in the narrative, and many of them sound important running motifs; but the sequence and emphasis of the overture do not correspond exactly to those of the narrative. Here are five consecutive items from the overture placed beside the passage they anticipate: the direct connections are indicated by italics.

A husky fifenote blew.

Blew. Blue bloom is on the

Gold pinnacled hair.

A jumping rose on satiny breasts of satin, rose of Castille.

With grace of alacrity towards the mirror gilt Cantrell and Cochrane's she turned herself. With grace she tapped a measure of gold whisky from her crystal keg. Forth from the skirt of his coat Mr Dedalus brought pouch and pipe. Alacrity she served. *He blew through the flue two husky fifenotes.*

—By Jove, he mused. I often wanted to see the Mourne mountains. Must be a great tonic in the air down there. But a long threatening comes at last, they say. Yes, yes.

Yes. He fingered shreds of hair, her maidenhair, her mermaid's, into the bowl. Chips. Shreds. Musing. Mute.

None not said nothing. Yes.

Gaily Miss Douce polished a tumbler,

Trilling, trilling:
Idolores (U 252).

trilling:
—*O, Idolores, queen of the eastern seas!*
—Was Mr Lidwell in today?
In came Lenehan. Round him peered
Lenehan. Mr Bloom reached Essex bridge.
Yes, Mr Bloom crossed bridge of Yessex.
To Martha I must write. Buy paper. Daly's.
Girl there civil. Bloom. Old Bloom. *Blue
Bloom is on the rye* (U 257).

The sequence of motifs in the narrative passage differs significantly from the sequence of abbreviated entries. In the overture 'A husky fifenote blew' leads to 'Blue Bloom is on the rye' by way of a pun. And as preparation for Miss Douce's 'trilling' of *Idolores* Joyce inserts two references to Miss Kennedy and Miss Douce, the barmaids, which have no exact equivalent in the narrative, but are compounded of a half-dozen descriptive fragments scattered over four pages in the narrative. Furthermore, the rose on Miss Douce's blouse is joined with the pun on *Rose of Castille* made by Lenehan in *Aeolus* (U 133), thus anticipating a chain of associations important to our understanding of the episode.

Or again, in the following passage, the overture's anticipation of a narrative passage embodies a significant shift in emphasis and meaning.

And a call, pure, long and throbbing. Longindying call.

Decoy. Soft word. But look! The bright stars fade. O rose! Notes chirruping answer. Castille. The morn is breaking.

In drowsy silence gold bent on her page.
From the saloon *a call came, long in dying*. That was a tuningfork the tuner had that he forgot that he now struck. A call again. That he now poised that it now *throbbed*. You hear? *It throbbed, pure, purer, softly and softlier,* its buzzing prongs. *Longer in dying call.*
Pat paid for diner's popcorked bottle: and over tumbler tray and popcorked bottle ere he went he whispered, bald and bothered, with Miss Douce.

Jingle jingle jaunted jingling (U 252).

—*The bright stars fade.* . . .

A voiceless song sang from within, singing:

—. . . *the morn is breaking.*

A duodene of *birdnotes chirruped bright treble answer* under sensitive hands. Brightly the keys, all twinkling, linked, all harpsichording, called to a voice to sing the strain of dewy morn, of youth, of love's leave-taking, life's, love's morn.

—*The dewdrops pearl* . . .

Lenehan's lips over the counter lisped a low whistle *of decoy.*

—*But look this way,* he said, *rose of Castille.*

Jingle jaunted by the curb and stopped.

She rose and closed her reading, *rose of Castille.* Fretted forlorn, dreamily rose (U 260; italics added).

When we re-read this section of the overture in the light of the succeeding narrative our apprehension of Bloom's sorrow is intensified. The overture ignores the personages of the narrative passage—Lenehan, Miss Douce, Pat the waiter—and transforms the 'dying call' of the tuning fork into Bloom's lament for the death of his passion with Molly, the rose of Castille, who will soon be jingling the family bed with jaunty Blazes Boylan.

A close examination of the first two pages of the *Sirens* episode shows them to be more than just a selection of 'extracts', an enumeration of the episode's *leitmotifs*. The overture is a re-fashioning of the *leitmotifs* which gives the following narrative a special perspective and increases our understanding of the episode's structure. It also initiates the reader into the episode's distinctive 'overlapping' style, the repetition of suggestive phrases and running motifs through which Joyce seeks to simulate polyphony. One obvious example of this method is Joyce's repeated use in different contexts of the word 'jingle' (the sound of Boylan's jaunting-car and Bloom's bed) to establish a continuous awareness in the reader's mind of the connections between Bloom's external situation and internal fears. As the episode progresses the process of 'thickening' the narrative is intensified in an attempt to unite the major motifs. The following passage, taken from near the end of the chapter, combines a number of *leitmotifs*.

Near bronze from anear near gold from afar they chinked their clinking glasses all, brighteyed and gallant, before bronze Lydia's tempting last rose of summer, rose of Castille. First Lid, De, Cow, Ker, Doll, a fifth: Lidwell, Si Dedalus, Bow Cowley, Kernan and Big Ben Dollard (U 285).

At least four of the overture's phrases which were introduced earlier in the narrative are recapitulated in this passage: 'Bronze by gold', Miss Douce's 'jumping rose', 'rose of Castille', and 'Big Ben'. These have gathered significance through repetition in various contexts; here they are brought together and related to each other in a passage which 'expresses' the episode's musical nature by translating the names of the cronies into musical tones: 'Lid, De, Cow, Ker, Doll, a fifth'. Joyce wishes the reader to hear this paragraph as a single chord, the related motifs harmonizing with each other. But the consecutive nature of language forces him to present them in rapid succession.

One of the last entries in the overture provides a neat example of Joyce's interweaving of motifs:

Last rose Castille of summer left bloom I feel so sad alone (U 253).

This line is actually a compound of several motifs suggested earlier in the overture, and it anticipates important relationships in the narrative. A partial catalogue of its components would include: 'rose of Castille', an allusion to Lenehan's riddle ('What opera is like a railway line?') and its answer, *The Rose of Castille* (see U 133 & 252); Molly as a rose, a 'Flower of the mountain' at

Gibraltar (768); and the 'jumping rose' on Miss Douce's blouse (252 & 256). The extreme compression of this line, the 'interweaving' of motifs, reflects Joyce's movement toward simultaneous presentation; but he retains the integrity of the individual word, although conventional syntax has been abandoned.

The overture to *Sirens* is successful in many ways. It whets our interest by a mysterious juxtaposition of familiar and unfamiliar motifs, while its phonetic devices prepare us for the method of the episode. But it would be absurd to claim that this section can be fully understood before the succeeding narrative has been carefully studied, or that Joyce achieves the full impact of Wagnerian *leitmotifs*. E. R. Curtius objects to the opening section on these grounds:

The literary technic here employed is an exact transposition of the musical treatment of the *leitmotif*, the Wagnerian method. But there is this difference, that the musical *motif* is complete in itself and aesthetically satisfying; I can hear a Wagnerian *leitmotif* with enjoyment, even though I cannot place its allusion (Valhalla theme? Walsungen theme?). But the *word-motif*, unintelligible in itself, acquires a meaning only when I relate it to its context. . . . Joyce has deliberately ignored this essential difference between sounds and words, and, for this reason, his experiment is of questionable value.[39]

Although Curtius may overstate his case, his objections cannot be dismissed. In trying to atone musical and literary forms, Joyce weakened the rational structure of his prose, exalting secondary qualities ('suggestion' and 'sound-imitation') at the expense of full communication. The *Sirens* episode demonstrates the weaknesses of a compromise between the two arts.

We have tried to view the *Sirens* episode as a compendium of those phonetic and structural devices which Joyce uses in *Ulysses* to approximate the 'condition of music'. The entire novel is a museum of traditional literary techniques, and this particular episode exhibits most of the methods used by nineteenth and twentieth-century writers in their search for musical form. One is reminded of Pound's treatment of sound and rhythm in the

Cantos, or of the 'symphonic' verse attempted by some of the Imagist poets. But Joyce went beyond his contemporaries in exploring the possibilities of adapting music to literature, and the partial failure of *Sirens* did not halt his work. In *Finnegans Wake* he destroyed a convention still respected in *Ulysses*, turning the verbal unit into a polysemantic vehicle capable of producing polyphonic effects. In the *Wake* Joyce no longer tried to imitate musical forms, but created his own form through a specialized medium. *Finnegans Wake* is not 'like' music, it is a kind of music.

One of the most penetrating analyses of the radical techniques Joyce employed in *Finnegans Wake* is that of David Daiches. Daiches recognizes that the problem of 'simultaneity' discussed in the last chapter is central to Joyce's musical intent.

In *Ulysses* the identity of one thing with another was indicated by the different levels on which the story was simultaneously told. In *Finnegans Wake* Joyce employs different levels not only within the narrative as a whole but within each word. Joyce endeavors to use words like musical chords, saying several things at once in one instant, with no one meaning subordinated to any other. Completely discarding chronology, sequence in time, as a means of expression, he seeks to replace it by a more instantaneous method, substituting for a running melody a series of staccato chords—yet not entirely giving up the running melody, for the staccato chords themselves occur in time, and themselves constitute units in a sequence. If Joyce could coin one kaleidoscopic word with an infinite series of meanings, a word which said everything in one instant yet leaving its infinity of meanings reverberating and mingling in the mind, he would have reached his ideal. *Finnegans Wake*, for all its six hundred pages, is meant to be thought of as an instantaneous whole; the fact that the words follow each other and do not all exist in the same place at once is due, we feel, to the exigencies of the dimensions, to the inexorable laws of existence, which even Joyce cannot defeat.[40]

The compounding of words in *Finnegans Wake* followed a number of rigid self-imposed 'rules' which Joyce seldom violated. These rules were the creation of a rational mind and were pursued by rational methods; they distinguish Joyce's late work from the chaotic nonsense produced by those members of the *transition* group who espoused the 'Revolution of the Word' and the 'Language of Night'. One of these 'rules' is that the various components of a portmanteau word must have an explicable relationship to each other, and must combine to create a unified effect which is appropriate to the context. Another is that the original or 'base' words must not be completely obscured in the process of deformation.

Joyce's method of constructing portmanteau words may be illustrated by an examination of the unit 'papacocopotl' in the following passage, taken from the schoolroom episode of the *Wake* (II. ii).

Docetism and Didicism, Maya-Thaya. Tamas-Rajas-Sattvas.

Match of a matchness, like your Bigdud dadder in the boudeville song, *Gorotsky Gollovar's Troubles*, raucking his flavourite turvku in the smukking precincts of lydias,[2] with Mary Owens and Dolly Monks seesidling to edge his cropulence and Blake-Roche, Kingston and Dockrell auriscenting him from afurz, our papacocopotl,[3] Abraham Bradley King? (ting ting! ting ting!) By his magmasine fall. Lumps, lavas and all.[4]

[2] A vagrant need is a flagrant weed.
[3] Grand for blowing off steam when you walk up in the morning.
[4] At the foot of Bagnabun Banbasday was lost on one (FW 294).

'Papacocopotl' is a sophisticated pun which relies on associations of sight and sound to communicate 'an emotional and intellectual complex in an instant of time.' At least four major components can be isolated:

papa   (Joyce's hero, HCE, is all fathers)
Popocatepetl   (HCE is identified with all mountains)

coco ('cocoa': In the *Wake* this is the body of the god, and suggests HCE in his sacramental role)

pot (A vulgar reminder of HCE's indiscretion in Phoenix Park. The entire word, 'papacocopotl', suggests his guilt stammer)

These four 'levels' within the portmanteau word express related aspects of HCE's nature, but the exactness of Joyce's method extends beyond the isolated unit. In context, 'papacocopotl' is intimately connected with its neighbours. HCE's position as paternal leader (God the Father) is reinforced by the reference to 'Bigdud dadder'; by the inclusion of 'Abraham Bradley King', once Lord Mayor of Dublin; and by 'cropulence', which suggests the life-giving nature of HCE's body. The identification with all mountains, especially volcanoes, is echoed in 'Lumps, lavas and all'. The remainder of the complex passage is composed of numerous allusions to HCE's original guilt as related in the 'boudeville' song (*boue de ville*, filth of the town). Swift, the two sluts, the three soldiers who spied on HCE from 'afurz', and Humpty Dumpty who fell from the Magazine Wall—all these allusions illuminate HCE's rôle as guilt-ridden, fallen hero.

The mechanics of this passage should indicate both the virtues and the limitations of Joyce's final method. In breaking down the structure of words he overcame what had been considered an insuperable barrier to the simulation of musical form—the linear nature of language. But the costs he paid for this freedom were enormous. Narrative structure disappeared, and with it the elements of suspense and action. Moreover, the total form of *Finnegans Wake* lacks the precision and inevitability displayed by a major musical composition. The 'simultaneity' which marks any passage from the *Wake* can only be grasped after an immense labour of exegesis, not only on that passage but on the entire work. An apprehension of Joyce's polyphony is limited to those who are familiar with his method and the *Wake's* basic patterns. *Finnegans Wake* is not properly music at all but poetry of the kind

Mallarmé envisaged, which reduces '*la durée à une division spiri-tuelle propre au sujet*'. In succeeding chapters we shall see how Joyce spent sixteen years fashioning a unique work of art that achieves—although at great cost—effects previously thought alien to literature.

NOTES FOR SECTION II

1. *Letters*, 146–47. JJ to Carlo Linati, 21 Sept. 1920.

2. L. A. G. Strong, *The Sacred River*, London, 1949, p. 144.

3. I borrow the term from Yvor Winters, although my attitude toward the technique differs radically from his. See *In Defense of Reason*, New York, 1947, pp. 60–64.

4. *Letters*, 135. JJ to Frank Budgen, 3 Jan. 1920.

5. *Letters*, 159. JJ to Frank Budgen, Feb. 1921.

6. *Letters*, 170. JJ to Frank Budgen, 16 Aug. 1921. Gorman (p. 281) substitutes 'he' for 'because' as one of the key words.

7. *Lotus-eaters* was published in the *Little Review*, V (July 1918), 37–49; *Aeolus*, V (Oct. 1918), 26–51.

8. Slocum, 138, item E. 5. a.

9. *Letters*, 172. JJ to HSW, 7 Oct. 1921.

10. *Little Review*, V (July 1918), 37–38. This version is substantially the same as that found in the Rosenbach MS.

11. *Ibid.*, 43. This version is substantially the same as that found in the Rosenbach MS.

12. Rosenbach MS. The last clause was omitted from the *Little Review* version, presumably at the request of the New York printer.

13. *Letters*, 172. JJ to HSW, 7 Oct. 1921.

14. See Stuart Gilbert, *James Joyce's 'Ulysses'*, New Edn., London, 1952, p. 183.

15. *Ibid.*, 191–95.

16. *Little Review*, V (Oct. 1918), 26.

17. *Ibid.*, p. 32. This version is substantially the same as that found in the Rosenbach MS.

18. *Counter-Statement*, New York, 1931, p. 171.

19. *Literary Essays of Ezra Pound*, ed. T. S. Eliot, London, 1954, p. 4. First published in *Poetry*, March 1913, under the title 'A Few Don'ts'.

20. For the complex history of the 'Imagist' movement, see Stanley K. Coffman, Jr., *Imagism*, Norman, Oklahoma, 1951.

21. It is interesting to note that Fenollosa's essay appeared in the *Little Review* while *Ulysses* was being serialized (Sept.–Dec. 1919).

22. *ABC of Reading*, London, 1951, p. 19.

23. *Ibid.*, p. 22.

24. *A Portrait of the Artist as a Young Man*, New York, The Modern Library, 1928, p. 249.

25. *Ibid.*, p. 250.

26. *Personae*, New Directions, 1926, p. 108.

27. Budgen, 156.

28. Joseph Frank, 'Spatial Form in Modern Literature', in *Critiques and Essays in Criticism*, ed. R. W. Stallman, New York, 1949, p. 325. Frank's essay, founded on Lessing's distinction between the arts of time and space, is a brilliant study of several problems discussed in this chapter.

29. *The Wound and the Bow*, Revised Edn., London, 1952, p. 236.

30. Frank, p. 328.

31. *Axel's Castle*, New York, 1950, p. 210.

32. Frank, p. 320.

33. *Letters of Ezra Pound*, ed. D. D. Paige, London, 1951, p. 247.

34. See *Letters*, 295.

35. *Oeuvres Complètes de Stéphane Mallarmé*, Gallimard, 1945, p. 654.

36. For an excellent discussion of musical form in modern literature, see 'The Analogy with Music' in Melvin Friedman's *Stream of Consciousness: A Study in Literary Method*, New Haven, 1955.

37. From 'The Music of Poetry', in *Selected Prose*, ed. John Hayward, London, 1953, p. 67.

38. *James Joyce's 'Ulysses'*, New Edn., London, 1952, p. 239.

39. *Ibid.*, 239–40. Translated from *Neue Schweizer Rundschau*, XXII (Jan. 1929).

40. David Daiches, *The Novel and the Modern World*, Chicago, 1939, pp. 148–149. One of the best—and least known—discussions of Joyce's syntax in the *Wake* is Margaret Schlauch, 'The Language of James Joyce', *Science and Society*, III (Fall 1939), 482–97.

III

WORK IN PROGRESS

1. EXPLORATION, 1923–26

WHEN *Finnegans Wake* first appeared in 1939 most readers familiar with *Ulysses* were confounded by what seemed to be a radical change in Joyce's style and technique. Superficially, the dense language of the *Wake* bore little resemblance to even the most complex sections of *Ulysses*. Only those who had studied the fragments of Joyce's *Work in Progress* published during the 1920's and 1930's[1] were prepared for the new language, realizing that it had developed gradually and inevitably out of the method of *Ulysses*. Today we are in a much better position to understand the affinities between *Ulysses* and *Finnegans Wake*, since the manuscript drafts and galley proofs of Joyce's last work provide complete and detailed evidence for every stage in the process of composition.[2] Using this material as a foundation, we shall attempt—in Henry James's words—'to remount the stream of composition' and trace the growth of *Finnegans Wake*.

Over a year passed after the publication of *Ulysses* before Joyce could muster the strength and determination to begin a new work. When the *Wake* was finally begun, in the spring of 1923, neither the structure nor the ultimate style of the book had been determined. Of course, Joyce had been preoccupied for years with many of the *Wake*'s major themes and motifs. The philosophies of Giordano Bruno and Giambattista Vico, which support the *Wake*'s structure, were familiar to Joyce from his early reading in Dublin and Trieste,[3] while some of the book's fundamental motifs (HCE's encounter with the Cad, the story of Buckley and the Russian General) belonged to the lore of the Joyce family.[4]

Many of the *Wake*'s important themes are foreshadowed in *Ulysses*, most notably Vico's cyclic view of history.[5] But although the materials of the *Wake* had been accumulating in his imagination since childhood, the manner in which this ripening vision would be presented was still not clear when Joyce began work in 1923. The early years of *Work in Progress* were exploratory, and Joyce's first efforts reveal a search for some dominant structure and a gradual clarification of stylistic aims.

It seems likely that Joyce spent most of 1922 reviewing his previous achievements and waiting for his principal interests to 'fuse' into a new form.[6] Certainly the collection and ordering of material was never completely abandoned. But if we have to choose an official date for the beginning of *Work in Progress* it must be 10 March 1923. On March 11th Joyce sent a letter to Harriet Weaver informing her that 'Yesterday I wrote two pages —the first I have written since the final *Yes* of *Ulysses*'.[7] These two pages were the earliest version of the 'King Roderick O'Conor' piece, now pages 380–82 of *Finnegans Wake*. On July 19th Joyce sent them to Harriet Weaver for typing, and then began sorting out his notes in preparation for future work. During the summer of 1923 he wrote three more sketches which were eventually incorporated into widely separated sections of the *Wake*: 'Tristan and Isolde' (now part of FW II. iv), 'St. Kevin' (FW 604–06), and 'pidgin fella Berkeley' (FW 611–12). In August Harriet Weaver typed these three pieces for Joyce, along with the 'King Roderick O'Conor' sketch.[8]

These four early fragments, which were revised and incorporated into the *Wake* late in the process of composition, indicate the nature of Joyce's mature method. Instead of following a narrative sequence and beginning with a draft of the *Wake*'s first episode (which actually was not written until 1926), he first explored four of his major interests: the artistic possibilities of Irish history (King Roderick O'Conor), the seduction motif (Tristan and Isolde), the figure of Shaun (St. Kevin), and the argument between St. Patrick and the archdruid. The last of these sketches is extremely significant. When Frank Budgen failed to take the 'pidgin fella Berkeley' passage seriously Joyce wrote to him:

Much more is intended in the colloquy between Berkely the arch-druid and his pidgin speech and Patrick in answer and his Nippon English. It is also the defence and indictment of the book itself, B's theory of colour and Patrick's practical solution of the problem.[9]

The druid defends in obscure terms the language and design of *Finnegans Wake*, borrowing his arguments from Berkeley's subjective theory of vision, but common-sense Patrick dismisses the druid's reasoning and with it the night-world of the *Wake*. It was almost inevitable that this passage, which ultimately found its place near the end of the *Wake*, should have been one of the first written. Joyce in writing it seems to have been debating with himself the advantages and disadvantages of the task he was about to undertake.

On 2 August 1923 Joyce, who was then vacationing in Sussex, sent Harriet Weaver three early drafts of the 'pidgin fella Berkeley' episode.[10] By comparing these versions we can gain some measure of his stylistic aims at the outset of *Work in Progress*. In the first version the archdruid explains his theory of colour in an abstract style less complex than that found in many parts of *Ulysses*. Here is the opening sentence:

The archdruid then explained the illusion of the colourful world, its furniture, animal, vegetable and mineral, appearing to fallen men under but one reflection of the several iridal gradations of solar light, that one which it had been unable to absorb while for the seer beholding reality, the thing as in itself it is, all objects showed themselves in their true colours, resplendent with the sextuple glory of the light actually retained within them.[11]

This first draft was cast into 'pidgin English' during a series of revisions. The 'final' 1923 draft opens as follows:

Bymby topside joss pidgin fella Berkeley, archdruid of Irish chinchinjoss, in the his heptachromatic sevenhued septicoloured roranyellgreeblindigan mantle finish he show along the his mister guest Patrick with alb belonga him the whose throat he fast all time what tune all him monkafellas with Patrick he drink up words all too much illusiones of hueful panepiphanal world of lord Joss the of which zoantholithic furniture from mineral through vegetal to animal not appear to full up together fallen man than under but one photoreflection of the several iridals gradationes of solar light that one which that part of it (furnit of huepanepi world) had shown itself (part of fur of huepamvor) unable to absorbere whereas for numpa one seer in seventh degree of wisdom of Entis-Onton he savvy inside true inwardness of reality, tha Ding hvad in idself id ist, all objects (of panepiwor) alloside showed themselves in trues coloribus resplendent with sextuple gloria of light actually retained inside them (obs of epiwo).[12]

Comparison of the two versions of the passage reveals several important characteristics of Joyce's method. As in *Ulysses* the revisions are expansive, an elaboration of the basic text. The names 'Berkeley' and 'Patrick' have been introduced in the final draft, but more important the language has been turned into Pidgin English so as to 'express' Joyce's conviction that early Irish religion was Eastern in nature. This process was continued in 1938, when Joyce re-worked the final 1923 version of this sentence for inclusion in Part IV of the *Wake* (611/4–24). He added allusions to several themes developed after 1923: the passage in *Finnegans Wake* opens with 'Tunc.', a reference to the 'TUNC' page of *The Book of Kells*, whose design Joyce felt was analogous to his own method. 'Berkeley' was also changed to 'Balkelly' in 1938, to remind the reader of 'Buckley' (who shot the Russian General). But these changes were not extensive, and the general level of allusiveness and compression achieved in 1923 met Joyce's exacting standards of fifteen years later. In the revisions of 'pidgin fella Berkeley' made during July 1923 one can see Joyce moving toward an extension of certain technical goals already evident in the writing of *Ulysses*.

In August and September of 1923 Joyce turned from the four brief sketches already discussed to the composition of 'Mamalujo' (*Ma*tthew-*Ma*rk-*Lu*ke-*Jo*hn), an episode in which the Four Old Men witness the honeymoon of Tristram and Isolde (now FW II. iv). On October 17th Joyce wrote to Harriet Weaver that 'Mamalujo' was 'finished but I am filing the edges off it'.[13] This 'filing process', as usual, took more time than Joyce had anticipated, and he was still revising 'Mamalujo' in the weeks before it was published in Ford Madox Ford's *Transatlantic Review* (April 1924).[14] 'Mamalujo' was the first section of *Work in Progress* to be published; in 1938 it was amalgamated with the 'Tristan and Isolde' sketch to form the final version of II. iv.[15]

During the early months of work on his new book Joyce felt compelled to justify in his letters the obscurity and fragmentary nature of his first sketches, which contrasted sharply with his early work on *Ulysses* 'where at least the ports of call were known beforehand.'[16] In 1923 the ultimate structure of *Work in Progress* was still unclear, and Joyce had no narrative framework such as the *Odyssey* to follow. Therefore he adopted the technique of getting the book's major figures and motifs on paper as quickly as possible, feeling that these were 'not fragments but active elements' which would 'begin to fuse of themselves' in time.[17] His favourite analogy for this mode of composition was that of an engineer boring into a mountain from different sides. 'I want to get as many sketches done or get as many boring parties at work as possible', he told Harriet Weaver.[18] Later he used the same analogy in speaking to August Suter: 'I am boring through a mountain from two sides. The question is, how to meet in the middle'.[19]

But although Joyce ranged widely in making his preliminary sketches for the *Wake*, he never lost sight of the family situation which lies at the centre of the work. By the middle of October 1923 he had drafted the first pages of I. ii., which review the origins of Humphrey Chimpden Earwicker's name and reputation. [20] This fragment (now FW 30–34) eventually reached print in the *Contact Collection of Contemporary Writers*, published in Paris in the spring of 1925. By the beginning of 1924 Joyce had filled a red-backed notebook with rough drafts of all the episodes of Part I except i and vi; this notebook was used as the basis for several fair copies of these episodes made in the first three months of 1924.[21] The drafts contained in the notebook reveal how far advanced Joyce's conception of Part I was, and show him in full possession of his major types—Earwicker, Anna Livia, the antithetical twins, and the young daughter. The fundamental themes of guilt and resurrection, as well as the technique of metamorphosing a number of personages into a single type, are prominent in these early drafts.

The opening months of 1924 found Joyce rapidly filling-out the chapters of Part I already drafted. A fair copy of the 'Hen' piece (I. v) was finished in January; more material was added to Shem (I. vii) in February; and on March 7th Joyce completed a fair copy of *Anna Livia* (I. viii).[22] Yet in spite of the firm grasp of themes and types displayed in the fair copy of *Anna Livia*, these early episodes for Part I were to undergo extensive revision before they found their place in *Finnegans Wake*. Every fragment of *Work in Progress* was subjected to a series of revisions which surpassed in scope and intensity the last-minute expansions of *Ulysses*.

There is no indication that Joyce had visualized as early as 1924 the basic four-part structure of the *Wake*, or that he thought of the early drafts in the red-backed notebook as belonging to a single unit. In March 1924 he began work on 'Shaun the Post' (now FW Part III), which was originally conceived as one piece but later expanded into four sections or 'watches', and work on Shaun occupied much of his time during 1924–25. There is some indication in an unpublished letter to Harriet Weaver that Joyce thought of Shaun as belonging with the pieces already drafted concerning HCE, Anna Livia and Shem, and that these were intended to form a second section of the *Wake* to follow a first section as yet unwritten.[23] But as work on Shaun progressed through 1924 the problems of structure became more rather than less complex. On November 9th Joyce announced the solution to one problem:

I think that at last I have solved one—the first—of the problems presented by my book. In other words one of the partitions between two of the tunnelling parties seems to have given way.[24]

The nature of this first problem, and its solution, are obscure; the union of the two tunnelling parties led only to more confusion.

[I am] pulling down more earthwork. The gangs are now hammering on all sides. It is a bewildering business.[25]

The composition of 'Shaun the Post', expanded by this time into four 'watches', continued through 1925, interrupted from time to time by the need for revising earlier episodes before their magazine publication. In April Joyce was rewriting 'The Hen' (I. v) for inclusion in the July *Criterion*, and encountering great difficulties.[26] A month later, in spite of serious trouble with his eyes, he was correcting proofs of the first pages of I. ii for the *Contact Collection of Contemporary Writers*, edited by Robert McAlmon: 'I have some proofs to correct for Mr McAlmon', Joyce wrote to Harriet Weaver on April 25th, 'and I had better do it before the other eye gets disabled'.[27] Later in the year he had to prepare an early version of *Anna Livia Plurabelle* for publication in the October issue of *Le Navire d'Argent*, and the Shem episode (I. vii) for the combined Autumn-Winter issue of *This Quarter*.

By the end of August 1925 Joyce had begun the fourth 'watch' of Shaun, and on October 10th he wrote:

I began [Shaun] d (otherwise the last watch of Shaun) a few days ago and have produced about three foolscapes of hammer and tongs stratification lit up by a fervent prayer to the divinity which shapes our roads in favour of my ponderous protagonist and his minuscule consort.[28]

The 'stratification' of Shaun d continued through the last months of 1925, and a first draft was finished sometime in November.

In the winter of 1925–26 Joyce's work was delayed by an eye operation, but the spring of 1926 found him revising the four 'watches' of Shaun as a unit. In April they were 'finished' and sent to the typist. The completion of 'Shaun the Post' seems to have acted as a catalyst on Joyce's imagination, for his letters of the succeeding two months reveal the final plan of the work crystallizing in his mind. On 21 May 1926 he wrote to Harriet Weaver:

I have the book now fairly well planned out in my head. I am as yet uncertain whether I shall start on the twilight games of ⊏, ∧ and ⊣ [Shem, Shaun and Issy] which will follow immediately after △ [Anna Livia] or on K[evin]'s orisons, to follow ∧ d [the last watch of Shaun].[29]

Early in the next month Joyce elaborated further on the episodes to follow *Anna Livia* (I. viii):

Between the close of △ [Anna Livia] at nightfall and ∧a [the first watch of Shaun, III. i] there are three or four other episodes, the children's games, night studies, a scene in the 'public', and a 'lights out in the village'.[30]

These two quotations show that by mid-1926, with a draft of Part III and a good deal of Part I already in hand, Joyce had solved most of his major structural problems and determined the final sequence of episodes. He had clearly visualized the four sections of Part II (the children's games, night studies, a scene in the 'public', and a 'lights out in the village') that were to be inserted between *Anna Livia* (I. viii) and the four 'watches' of Shaun (Part III). These episodes are a necessary 'bridge' between the heroic dimensions of Part I and the disintegration of the hero in the Shaun of Part III; they connect the past with the future, for in Part II the present-day companions of Earwicker and his wife —their children, the Twelve Citizens and the Four Old Men— rehearse the themes of the book. With the planning of this transitional section Joyce had conquered his major problem of composition. At approximately the same time he foresaw a concluding section which would include Kevin's orisons and follow as a Coda after the four 'watches' of Shaun.

With the plan for Part II now clearly before him, Joyce wrote in the summer of 1926 a piece called 'The Triangle', which later became 'The Muddest Thick That Was Ever Heard Dump' in *Tales Told of Shem and Shaun* (1929) and the middle of the classroom episode (II. ii) in *Finnegans Wake*.[31] After finishing this fragment he paused to assess his position:

> I have done a piece of the studies, Ⴑ [Shem] coaching ∧ [Shaun] how to do Euclid Bk I, 1. I will do a few more pieces, perhaps ⊣ [Issy's] picture-history from the family album and parts of O [the twelve] discussing A Pai (I would like to invent a satisfactory fountain pen!) *A Painful Case* and the ⊓–Δ [Earwicker-Anna Livia] household etc.[32]

This letter shows Joyce well into the planning of Part II. The 'piece of the studies' mentioned is found in the same notebook with the fourth part of Shaun (III. iv), and at the end of this 1926 notebook we find the first draft of *Finnegans Wake* I. i.[33] Joyce composed this initial chapter with special care, aware of its crucial position in the *Wake*'s structure; therefore we are justified in using it as a measure of his technical development during the years of exploratory writing (1923–26).

In 1926 Joyce asked Harriet Weaver to 'order' an episode by sending him some material which she would like to see incorporated in the *Wake*. Knowing his preoccupation with the prehistoric aspects of HCE, Miss Weaver responded by mailing Joyce a pamphlet on St. Andrew's Church, Penrith, which mentioned a fabulous 'giant' supposedly buried in the churchyard. After receiving the pamphlet Joyce began to adapt it and could soon reply:

> I set to work at once on your esteemed order and so hard indeed that I almost stupefied myself and stopped, reclining on a sofa and reading

Gentlemen Prefer Blondes for three whole days. But this morning I started off afresh. I am putting the piece in the place of honour, namely the first pages of the book. Will try to deliver same punctual by Xmas. . . . The book really has no beginning or end. (Trade secret, registered at Stationers Hall.) It ends in the middle of a sentence and begins in the middle of the same sentence.[34]

Seven days later, on November 15th, Joyce sent Miss Weaver an early version of the first paragraph accompanied by an extended commentary.[35]

Between the inception of the *Wake*'s first paragraph in late 1926 and its publication in *transition* for April 1927 Joyce lavished many hours of correction and revision upon it. The earliest version is covered with marginal and interlinear additions; I shall quote it first as it was originally written, and then as it appears after the corrections and additions are included.

Howth Castle & Environs! Sir Tristram had not encore arrived from North Armorica nor stones exaggerated themselves in Laurens county, Ga, doubling all the time, nor a voice answered mishe chishe to tuff-tuff thouartpatrick. Not yet had a kidscalf buttended an isaac not yet had twin sesthers played siege to twone jonathan. Not a peck of malt had Shem and Son brewed & bad luck to the regginbrew was to be seen on the waterface

brings us to Howth Castle & Environs! Sir Tristram violer d'amores, had passencore rearrived on a merry isthmus from North Armorica to wielderfight his peninsular war, nor sham rocks by the Oconee exaggerated themselse to Laurens county, Ga, doubling all the time, nor a voice from afire bellowsed mishe chishe to tufftuff thouartpeatrick. Not yet though venisoon after had a kidscad buttended a bland old isaac not yet [though] all's fair in vanessy were sosie sesthers wroth with twone jonathan. Rot a peck of pa's malt had Jhem or Sen brewed by arclight & rory end to the regginbrow was to be seen ringsome on the waterface[36]

After undergoing several further revisions the opening paragraph appeared in *transition* as follows:

riverrun brings us back to Howth Castle & Environs. Sir Tristram, violer d'amores, fr' over the short sea, had passencore rearrived from North Armorica on this side the scraggy isthmus of Europe Minor to wielderfight his penisolate war: nor had topsawyer's rocks by the stream Oconee exaggerated themselse to Laurens County's gorgios, while they went doublin their mumper all the time; nor avoice from afire bellowsed mishe mishe to tauftauf thuartpeatrick: not yet, though venissoon after, had a kidscad buttended a bland old isaac; not yet, though all's fair in vanessy, were sosie sesthers wroth with twone nathandjoe. Rot a peck of pa's malt had Jhem or Shen brewed by arclight and rory end to the regginbrow was to be seen ringsome on the waterface[37]

With the exception of 'waterface' being replaced by 'aquaface', the only changes between this version and that which opens *Finnegans Wake* occurred in the first sentence, which reads in the *Wake*:

riverrun, past Eve and Adam's, from swerve of shore to bend of bay, brings us by a commodius vicus of recirculation back to Howth Castle and Environs.

Every important theme sounded in the final version of the opening paragraph is present in the earliest draft of the passage, and some are expressed in forms close to the final text. As usual, revision was primarily an elaboration of the basic form. In the earliest draft the geographical presence of HCE dominates the Dublin scene in 'Howth Castle & Environs!' The circular structure of 'the book of Doublends Jined' is evident in the immediate revision of the first sentence, where 'brings us to' is obviously a continuation of a concluding sentence already planned. By the *transition* version this has been expanded into 'riverrun brings us back to', thus introducing the Liffey's place in the cyclic plan of the book and emphasizing the fluid nature of Joyce's work. The words 'brings us back to', along with the change of 'arrived' to 'rearrived' in the revision of the first draft, imply that the cycles of the book are repetitions of archetypal cycles.

During the early development of the opening passage additional phrases were inserted to 'thicken' the fundamental motifs. 'By arclight', inserted into the first draft, prepares the way for succeeding references to Noah's rainbow, while 'topsawyer's' in the *transition* text suggests Tom Sawyer as the American counterpart of Shaun, the dominant brother. Even the smallest changes are significant: 'doubling' appears in *transition* as 'doublin' to remind the reader that the process being described is a universal one, as true of Dublin as of Georgia; and 'thouartpatrick' is altered to 'thouartpeatrick' so as to introduce an Irish 'peat rick'.

A more extended example of this 'stratification' is found in the development of the Swift-Stella-Vanessa motif through the early versions.

. . . not yet had twin sesthers played siege to twone jonathan.	. . . not yet [though] all's fair in vanessy were sosie sesthers wroth with twone jonathan.	. . . not yet, though all's fair in vanessy, were sosie sesthers wroth with twone nathandjoe.

Here the additions amplify the original theme. 'Vanessy' suggests Vanessa. 'Sosie' replaces 'twin' as a combination of 'saucy' and 'Susannah'; 'wroth' hints at Ruth; Esther was already present in 'sesthers'; and the authors of the *Skeleton Key to 'Finnegans Wake'* remind us that the Biblical stories of Susannah, Ruth and Esther, like that of Swift and his two lovers, involve 'the loves of old men for young girls'.[38] 'Nathandjoe', which replaces 'jonathan' in the *transition* version, 'is an anagram for Jonathan (Dean Jonathan Swift) split in two and turned head over heels by his two young-girl loves, Stella and Vanessa'.[39]

Joyce's skilful shaping of this passage indicates that by late 1926 the density which characterizes the final text of *Finnegans Wake* was already his ideal, and that he could achieve it with complete confidence. The years 1926–27 marked a turning point in the evolution of the *Wake*. From this point on Joyce was working to a clearly visualized structural pattern, and aiming for linguistic effects that he had already fully mastered in scattered passages. The remaining twelve years of laborious composition were given over to completing the design and recasting the entire work in his achieved 'final' style. This period could best be described, in the words of the young Stephen Dedalus, as years of 'slow elaborative patience'.[40]

2. SLOW ELABORATIVE PATIENCE, 1927-39

Between 1927 and 1930 Joyce published advanced versions of the first and third Parts of *Finnegans Wake* in the *avant-garde* magazine *transition*. Although he did not share many of the radical theories held by *transition*'s editors and contributors, and remained aloof from most of the 'movements' and 'manifestoes' supported by the magazine, he welcomed the opportunity to revise the major portion of his early work for publication. Without the stimulus provided by the *transition* deadlines it is doubtful if Joyce would have ever finished the *Wake* in its present form. During 1927 the earliest complete version of Part I was published serially in the first eight issues of the new journal. The first chapter, which appeared in the April issue, was so well liked by the editors that Joyce agreed to fill in the gaps that still existed in Part I.[41] He joined the section already published in the *Contact Collection of Contemporary Writers* (FW 30-34) with the episode that had appeared in the *Criterion* (FW 104-25) by 'finishing off' the intervening two episodes, which had been drafted in 1923-24. He then found it necessary to connect 'The Hen' (I. v) with 'Shem the Penman' (I. vii) by a new episode which was composed at high speed and under great pressure.[42] Meanwhile all the previously published episodes were revised and expanded for their appearance in *transition*. Finally in November 1927 the eighth chapter appeared and the first Part of *Work in Progress* was in print, running without a break from 'riverrun' to the close of *Anna Livia Plurabelle*. Future revisions of this Part may be classified as 'secondary', consisting in the extension of major themes and the inclusion of dependent motifs.

An interesting view of the manner in which Joyce collected material during the *transition* years (1927–38) is provided by Eugene Jolas:

We saw a good deal of him during those years. . . . All his friends collaborated then in the preparations of the fragments destined for *transition*: Stuart Gilbert, Padraic Colum, Elliot Paul, Robert Sage, Helen and Giorgio Joyce, and others. He worked with painstaking care, almost with pedantry. He had invented an intricate system of symbols permitting him to pick out the new words and paragraphs he had been writing down for years, and which referred to the multiple characters in his creation. He would work for weeks, often late at night, with the help of one or the other of his friends. It seemed almost a collective composition in the end, for he let his friends participate in his inventive zeal, as they searched through numberless notebooks with mysterious reference points to be inserted in the text. When finished, the proof looked as if a coal-heaver's sooty hands had touched it.[43]

The method described by Jolas is reminiscent of the late revisions to *Ulysses*. Continual embroidery upon a fixed pattern characterized Joyce's work on both *Ulysses* and the *Wake*; the only difference is that the process was carried on for a much longer period of time in the later work, and that Joyce abandoned the conventional structure of language to permit this further elaboration.

The year 1928 opened with the publication of 'The Triangle' (later 'The Muddest Thick That Was Ever Heard Dump', now FW 282–304) in the February issue of *transition*. Then Joyce turned to the four 'watches' of Shaun and began to revise them; they appeared in *transition* between March 1928 and November 1929. At the same time he was re-working *Anna Livia* for separate publication by Crosby Gaige in October.[44] Joyce had a great deal of trouble with his eyes during this period, and between June and October of 1928 he was able to write only one piece, 'a short description of madness and blindness descending upon Swift' which was never included in the *Wake*.

Unslow, malswift, pro mean, proh noblesse, Atrahora, Melancolores, nears; whose glauque eyes glitt bedimmd to imm! whose fingrings creep o'er skull: till, qwench! asterr mist calls estarr and grauw! honath John raves homes glowcoma.[45]

This passage mirrors Joyce's fear of blindness and madness which was accentuated by his ill health at the time, a fear that was to hamper the progress of his work more and more in the coming years. His letters contain frequent allusions to exhaustion and nervous strain, caused to some degree by his insistence on repeated and intensive revisions of each episode before publication. These last-minute changes often produced the added anxiety of delayed publication.

As soon as the proofs of the Crosby Gaige *Anna Livia* had been corrected in May 1928, Joyce began to concern himself with the revision of his three 'fables' which had already appeared in *transition* and were to comprise his next publication in book form: 'The Mookse and the Gripes' (FW 152–59), 'The Muddest Thick That Was Ever Heard Dump' (FW 282–304), and 'The Ondt and the Gracehoper' (FW 414–19).[46] The recasting of the fables extended well into the spring of 1929, and in August they appeared under the title *Tales Told of Shem and Shaun*.

In February 1929 the third 'watch' of Shaun was published in *transition* No. 15, and the fourth followed in November (*transition* No. 18), thus completing the initial publication of Part III. Part of the third watch was then revised for book publication, and came out in June 1930 under the title *Haveth Childers Everywhere* (now FW 532–54). In re-working this section Joyce utilized to full advantage his techniques of 'orchestration', creating more and more complex portmanteau words in his search for simultaneity of effect. This aim is exemplified in the 'stratification' of the following passage:

That was Communicator a former colonel. A disincarnated spirit called Sebastiam may phone shortly. Let us cheer him up a little and make an appointment for a future date. Hello, Communicate! how's the butts? Everseptic! ... So enjoying of old thick whiles, in tall white hat of four reflections he would puffout a smokefull bock.

[1929]

That was Communicator, a former Colonel. A disincarnated spirit, called Sebastion, from the Rivera in Januero, (he is not all hear) may fernspreak shortly with messuages from my deadported. Let us cheer him up a little and make an appunkment for a future date. Hello, Commudicate! How's the buttes? Everscepistic! ... So enjoying of old thick whiles, in haute white toff's hoyt of our formed reflections, with stock of eisen all his prop, so buckely hosiered from the Royal Leg, and his puertos mugnum. He would puffout a dhymful bock. [1930][47]

The revised text has been enriched with several geographical names: the Riviera and Rio de Janeiro ('Rivera in Januero'), Everest ('Everscepistic'), and Eisenstadt ('stock of eisen'). In the latter part of the passage HCE is a white-capped volcano; his snow-white head and smoking cigar are the mountain peak, while ports ('puertos mugnum') lie at his feet. This image has been foreshadowed in the second version by two revisions: the substitution of 'buttes' for 'butt', and the addition of 'deadported' (departed). 'Messuages', with its overtones of 'messages' and 'assuages', as well as its root meaning of 'house and lands', is a typical Joycean addition. 'Buckely hosiered' combines the image of buckled hose with a reference to Buckley (who shot HCE as the Russian General). The alteration of 'Everseptic' to 'Everscepistic' reflects a characteristic compression, for here three attributes of HCE have been merged into the original word. His identification with all mountains is in 'Everest'; he is a 'sceptic'; he is tainted—'septic'—and at the same time 'pistic', pure as the oil with which Mary anointed the feet of Jesus.

There can be no doubt that in revising this passage Joyce multiplied its references and enriched his text, but only at the expense of obscuring some of the original (and important) meanings: 'Everseptic' is overshadowed by the more complex 'Everscepistic'. Too often the process of deformation diffuses the basic effect instead of intensifying it; in many cases the earlier versions of a passage contain essential elements which are blurred in the final text. This is an inherent defect of Joyce's method.

In the late months of 1929, with Parts I and III of his work already in print, Joyce 'felt a sudden kind of drop' in the impetus behind his writing.[48] The constant strain of working to a schedule, coupled with his ill health, had left him completely exhausted. It was not until September 1930 that he could bring himself to begin work on the virtually untouched Part II.[49] With no deadlines to be met, the composition of II. i proceeded slowly. By November 22nd he had finished a 'first draft of about two thirds of the first section of Part II (2,200 words) which came out like drops of blood'.[50]

The nervous illness of Joyce's daughter, Lucia, which reached a crisis during 1931–32, caused a drastic reduction in the pace of his work. The composition of Part II advanced slowly and under great difficulties, interrupted by occasional revisions of Part I. The draft of II. i was finally completed in 1932, but somehow the MS. disappeared and Joyce spent the best part of November reconstructing it from notes and his memory.[51] The chapter finally appeared in February 1933 (*transition* No. 22).

Joyce's work of the 1930's may be distinguished from his earlier efforts by the complete control of his material that it exhibits. No longer was composition a process of exploration, a search for structural solutions or the perfection of linguistic devices. Instead the ultimate form of the book was fixed in his mind, and—as in the last stages of writing *Ulysses*—he elaborated like a mosaic worker upon a predetermined pattern. His friends of the time who were familiar with his methods, especially Louis Gillet and Eugene Jolas, have recorded their impressions of Joyce at work, and they attest that he held the incredibly complex form of the *Wake* in his mind as a single image, and could move from one section to another with complete freedom.[52] The first drafts made during the 1930's were much more comprehensive than those of the 1920's, since Joyce had a precise notion of each episode's final shape and its relationship to surrounding episodes. The number of cross-references added in revision became fewer, and were of less importance, for each successive episode was written against a background of greater accumulated material and with more 'finished' sections in mind.

If we compare the version of II. i which appeared in *transition* (February 1933) with the corresponding episode in *Finnegans Wake*, these alterations in Joyce's method will become clear. The 1933 text of II. i was enlarged to one-third again its original length before final publication, but the changes were almost entirely minor additions which enrich the narrative with secondary references but leave the original intent untouched. The initial phrasing usually remains the same and the additions are inserted between phrases which they expand or qualify.

For example, on page 232 of *Finnegans Wake* the outcast Glugg (Shem), having thrown a fit and danced a jig, is about to recover control of himself when a message arrives from Izod renewing his hopes. In the 1933 version this paragraph is already associated with Swift and his girl-lover Esther Johnson through the use of the 'little language' (Ppt, MD) in the last two sentences.

Stop up, mavrone, and sit in my lap. Pepette, though I'd much rather not. Like things are m. ds. is all in vincibles. Decoded.[53]

In the 1939 version the correspondence between Izod and Stella is further strengthened by additions to a sentence earlier in the paragraph describing the 'message' from Izod.

When a message interfering intermitting interskips from them on herzian waves, a butterfly from her zipclasped handbag, awounded dove astarted from, escaping out her forecotes.

transition (February 1933)[54]

When (pip!) a message interfering intermitting interskips from them (pet!) on herzian waves, (call her venicey names! call her a stell!) a butterfly from her zipclasped handbag, a wounded dove astarted from, escaping out her forecotes.

(FW 232/9–13)

Through these additions Izod becomes a star ('a stell') containing both Stella and Vanessa ('venicey'): the rival lovers are one in her. 'Venice' in 'venicey' also suggests *Othello*, another story of tragic love between a young girl and an older man. The children in their games are re-enacting the Swiftian archetype of frustrated love, reminding one of Earwicker's incestuous desire for Issy. The message from Izod is a *Journal to Stella* in reverse, framed in the same 'little language'. However, Izod is not only Stella-Vanessa but Swift as well, and the twins are masculine versions of the rival lovers: a similar reversal occurs later in the chapter when she becomes 'la pau' Leonie' (Napoleon) who 'has the choice of her lives between Josephinus and Mario-Louis', obviously Joséphine and Marie Louise (FW 246/16–17). But the important thing to notice about these revisions is that they do not add a new dimension to the passage but expand and refine allusions which are quite obvious in the 1933 version.

To obtain a clearer idea of Joyce's late revisions we must examine the expansion of a longer passage, such as the following from near the end of II. i. The children are returning home from their games, and at the conclusion of the quotation the door is slammed behind them with an echo of the hundred-letter thunderclap first heard in the third paragraph of the *Wake*. I have italicized those words added in the course of revision; the entire 1933 text was retained without alteration.

While, *running about their ways, going and coming, now at rhimba rhomba, now in trippiƷa trappaƷa, pleating a pattern Gran Geamatron showed them of gracehoppers, auntskippers and coneyfarm leppers,* they jeerilied along, *durian gay and marian maidcap, lou Dariou beside la Matieto, all boy more all girl singoutfeller longa house blong store Huddy,*

*whilest nin nin nin nin that Boorman's clock, a winny on the tinny side,
ninned nin nin nin nin,* about old Father Barley how he got up of a
morning arley and he met with a plattonem blondes named Hips and
Haws and fell in with a fellows of Trinity some header Skowood
Shaws like (*You'll catch it, don't fret, Mrs Tummy Lupton! Come
indoor, Scoffynosey, and shed your swank!*) auld Daddy Deacon who
could stow well his place of beacon but he never could hold his
kerosene's candle to (*The nurse'll give it you, stickypots! And you wait,
my lasso, fecking the twine!*) bold Farmer Burleigh who wuck up in a
hurlywurly where he huddly could wuddle to wallow his weg tillbag
of the baker's booth to beg of (*You're well held now, Missy Cheekspeer,
and your panto's off! Fie, for shame, Ruth Wheatacre, after all the booz
said!*) illed Diddiddy Achin for the prize of a pease of bakin *with a
pinch of the panch of the ponch in jurys* for (*Ah, crabeyes, I have you,
showing off to the world with that gape in your stocking!*) Wold For-
rester Farley who, *in deesperation of deispiration at the diasporation of
his diesparation,* was found of the round of the sound of the lound of
the. Lukkedoerendunandurraskewdylooshoofermoyportertooryzooy-
sphalnabortan*sporthaokan*sakroidverjkapakkapuk.[55]

The middle section of the thunder-word, 'fermoyporter', combines HCE's specific Dublin name (Porter) with *fermez la porte*
and a cry for more drink ('moyporter'). The additions to the
paragraph, which appear at first to be merely in the cause of
onomatopœia, actually embody a number of significant expansions. 'Trippiza trappaza' and 'rhimba rhomba' point forward to
'triv and quad' (FW 306/12) and the lessons of the twins in the
next episode, where Dolph helps Kev with a geometrical analysis
of the 'Gran Geamatron' mentioned in this passage. 'Gracehoppers, auntskippers and coneyfarm leppers'—the followers of
Glugg, Chuff and Izod—also foreshadow a later section, the fable
of 'The Ondt and the Gracehoper' (FW 414–419).

'Durian gay' relates the Glugg-Chuff antithesis to Oscar
Wilde's tale of dual personality, *The Picture of Dorian Gray,*
while simultaneously combining 'dour an' gay', the opposed
temperaments of the two brothers who are each one-half of
HCE's dual personality. The connection with Wilde himself is

also significant, since he figures elsewhere in the *Wake* as part of the homosexual motif. 'Marian maidcap' is, of course, the giddy Izod, who plays Maid Marian in the children's adventures.

Among the other allusions added by Joyce, the recurring groups of four elements ('nin nin nin nin', 'with a pinch of the panch of the ponch in jurys') culminating in the series 'in deesperation of deispiration at the diasporation of his diesparation' reinforce the four-part rhythm which precedes the thunderword in both versions: 'was found of the round of the sound of the lound of the'. The last of these four-part insertions can be identified by its '-ation' endings as a comment of the Twelve, the customers at Earwicker's pub. 'Deesperation' probably stems from the French *déesse* meaning 'goddess'. 'Deis' is an obsolete form of 'dais'; it introduces connotations of height and distinction, and suggests an elevated stage for acting. 'Diasporation' means 'fragmentation', specifically the Dispersion of the disobedient prophesied in the Old Testament (Deuteronomy xxviii. 25). And 'diesparation' reminds one of the *Dies irae* and the Last Judgment.

In the alphabetical sequence of these four words lies the plot of the episode: spurred on by the 'goddess' Izod, Glugg and Chuff strive to 'elevate' themselves in her eyes. Also, the machinery of the episode is that of a stage production. When the games break up, the children are 'dispersed' to their various homes, and the thunderclap which will accompany the Last Judgment is heard when the father of the twins slams the door behind them.

But the progress of the episode has also been along 'Vico's road', down which the children march (FW 246/25). The Divine age (*déesse*) is followed by the Heroic ('deis', the giants), which is in turn succeeded by the Dispersion of democracy and individualism, until the divine thunderclap ends the cycle and provides energy for 'recirculation': Omega becomes Alpha, New Zealand is replaced by Newer Aland, and the pattern is repeated. This presentation of Vico's scheme for the race is accompanied and paralleled by the individual cycle of Birth, Marriage, Death, and Resurrection. Thus Joyce's last insertion before the thunder-noise recapitulates the action of the chapter, relates it to the book's major philosophic theme, and explains the significance of the hundred-letter word that follows. Such was the multi-levelled condensation he aimed at in his later revisions. However, these late changes rarely add a new and significant dimension to the text; instead, they repeat and amplify elements of the basic narrative. Joyce's method was that of accretion, and such a method has no inherent boundaries. Often the final revisions enrich the text, but there are times when they lead to redundancy. Joyce's method, in its lack of discrimination and selection, reflects his ultimate purpose in the *Wake*, which was to make all his knowledge and experience implicit in the microcosmic life of a single family.

It is no coincidence that those who observed Joyce at work on *Finnegans Wake* often employ the same analogy that struck Frank Budgen while he watched the making of *Ulysses*, the analogy with mosaic-work. In a mosaic the basic outline is clear and simple, the individual pieces have fixed colours and dimensions. But within the intermediate divisions of the form the pieces are grouped according to less exact principles of design, and one piece can be exchanged for another similar unit without affecting the composition as a whole. In a like fashion, the intermediate divisions of the *Wake* are loosely-organized groups of associated items, and within their general context similar word-groups can be exchanged or moved about without greatly affecting the total impact of the passage. There is no inevitability to their placing.

The comparison with mosaic-work is illuminating, but it cannot be used as a justification for Joyce's final aesthetic aims. There is a crucial distinction between a composition in colour and line which can be viewed as a single image, and a composition in words which must be read over a period of time and united in retrospect. It is a commonplace of Joycean criticism to justify the techniques of *Finnegans Wake* by comparing them with early Celtic design, such as that found in the *Book of Kells*. Joyce encouraged this approach. Part of the chapter on ALP's 'Mamafesta' (FW 119–23) is a parody of Sir Edward Sullivan's description of the *Book of Kells*, as the authors of the *Skeleton Key to 'Finnegans Wake'* point out.[56] Joyce seems to have regarded the 'TUNC' page of that work, the incredibly involved illumination of Matthew xxvii. 38 (TUNC CRU—CIFIXERANT—XPI CUM EO DU—OS LATRONES), as having a special affinity with his own art: the word 'Tunc' introduces 'pidgin fella Balkelly's' (and Joyce's) defence of the *Wake* in Part IV (FW 611). The similarities between the two works are indeed striking. As Herbert Read has said, 'the closest analogy to the literary method of *Work in Progress* is perhaps to be found in the early graphic art of Joyce's own country, the abstract involved ornament of the Celts. Here is a very good description of such art by a German writer:

There are certain simple motives whose interweaving and commingling determines the character of this ornament. At first there is only the dot, the line, the ribbon; later the curve, the circle, the spiral, the zigzag, and an S-shaped decoration are employed. Truly, no great wealth of motives! But what variety is attained by the manner of their employment! Here they run parallel, then entwined, now latticed, now knotted, now plaited, then again brought through one another in a symmetrical checker of knotting and plaiting. Fantastically confused patterns are thus evolved, whose puzzle asks to be unravelled, whose convolutions seem alternatively to seek and avoid each other, whose component parts, endowed as it were with sensibility, captivate sight and sense in passionately vital movement.[57]

But no matter how close the parallels, the undoubted success of Celtic illumination cannot stand as authority for Joyce's interminable elaborations upon the basic themes of the *Wake*. Few readers would deny that the effects Joyce achieved by subjecting his early drafts to 'a series of gross exaggerations' are partially negated by the loss of that sense of inevitability which Harry Levin sees as 'the touchstone of a more reserved style'.[58]

Between 1932 and 1938 Part II of the *Wake* gradually took form. The first chapter was published separately in 1934 under the title *The Mime of Mick Nick and the Maggies*. The next year those portions of the schoolroom episode which surround 'The Muddest Thick That Was Ever Heard Dump' were published in *transition*, thus completing a version of II. ii. By February 1937 the first pages of II. iii (FW 309–31) were ready for publication, and the next year another large segment of II. iii was printed in *transition* (No. 27, April–May 1938).

The episode of the Twelve at the Tavern (II. iii), the longest and most complex in *Finnegans Wake*, was one of the last sections written. It stands at the physical centre of the *Wake* and serves a function similar to that of the *Circe* episode in *Ulysses*: most of the major motifs are recapitulated in it. It is interesting to note that the Tavern scene appears at approximately the same stage in the composition of the *Wake* as does *Circe* in the making of *Ulysses*. After *Circe* was completed only parts of the *Nostos* remained to be written, along with a general revision of the entire novel. After the Tavern scene had been constructed it only remained to combine the early 'Tristan and Isolde' fragment with 'Mamalujo', thus forming II. iv; to complete the concluding Part IV; and to tighten up the work as a whole.[59] In *Work in Progress*, as in the making of *Ulysses*, Joyce composed from both ends at once, finally drawing the two halves together in a scene of transformation and recapitulation. We might compare those early (1923) fragments which ultimately found their place in Part IV of the *Wake* ('St. Kevin' and 'pidgin fella Berkeley') with the 'preliminary sketches for the final sections' of *Ulysses* that Joyce is said to have made early in 1914.[60]

Joyce began to prepare *Finnegans Wake* for book publication in 1936, when he revised the latest printed text of Part I for submission to Faber and Faber.[61] The next year the galleys for Part I were ready: the sheet for the first page of the *Wake* bears the printer's date '12 March 1937'.[62] The fact that the book was being printed in England increased the difficulty of correcting proof, as did Joyce's habit of making extensive revisions on successive sets of galleys. During 1938 the proof sheets poured in while he was still composing Part IV. It was not until mid-November that the last words of the book were written, and final revisions were made after this. Louis Gillet remembers that corrections were being sent by telegram up to the very last moment.[63] Although the trade edition of *Finnegans Wake* did not appear until 4 May 1939, Joyce received the first bound copy in time for his fifty-seventh birthday celebration on February 2nd, when he revealed the title that he had jealously guarded for so long.[64] Sixteen years of exploration and elaboration had ended.

3. THE EVOLUTION OF *ANNA LIVIA PLURABELLE*

The making of *Anna Livia Plurabelle* (FW I. viii) was more complex than that of any other episode, and more significant in revealing the development of Joyce's art during those years when *Finnegans Wake* was known only as *Work in Progress*. Among the first of the episodes to be conceived, *Anna Livia* went through seventeen distinct stages of revision between 1923 and 1938.[65] It appeared in more printed versions than any other section, and became for the reading public the chief representative of Joyce's new work. Joyce's own fondness for the episode is reflected in his careful revisions, while his letters leave no doubt that he thought *Anna Livia* a triumph and justification for his experiments. Most critics would agree that his radical techniques are nowhere more successful, and anyone who hears Joyce's recording of the episode's close must be impressed by the marvellous union of subject and form.[66] Since the evolution of *Anna Livia* mirrors in miniature the growth of the entire *Wake*, an understanding of it should lead to a just estimate of Joyce's late methods.

The first and second drafts of *Anna Livia* must have been made in the winter of 1923–24; they are found in the famous red-backed notebook containing rough drafts of all the episodes in Part I except i and vi.[67] The earliest draft is a skeleton outline of the first half of the episode (now pp. 196–208 of the *Wake*). It opens in a manner close to the final form:

O tell me all now about Anna Livia. I want to know all about Anna Livia. Well, you know Anna Livia? Yes, of course, I know Anna. Tell me all. Tell me now. You'll die when you hear. Well, you see, when the old chap did what you know. Yes, I know, go on. Or whatever it was they try to make out he tried to do in Phoenix park. He's an awful old rep. . . .[68]

The paragraph divisions in this first draft are approximately the same as those in the final published version. Joyce appears to have sketched in his 'narrative' units as short paragraphs, and then expanded these through a series of revisions. For instance, the eighty-word paragraph on page 207 of *Finnegans Wake* which begins with 'Describe her! . . .' is only twenty-six words long in the first draft:

Describe her! I must hear that. What had she on? What did she carry? Here she comes. What has she got? A loin of jubilee mutton.[69]

Usually the basic outline of a paragraph remained the same throughout its growth. Joyce seems to have thought of his original units as fundamental designs which could be expanded indefinitely through his techniques of amplification. It should be noted that the original units are almost always 'narrative' in the conventional sense, whereas the revisions introduce analogies and connections which are essentially 'static'. Leon Edel was not far from the mark when he concluded, after examining several published versions of *Anna Livia*, that 'one is almost tempted to say . . . Joyce wrote the whole book out first in traditional form and then proceeded to translate it into the special idiom he devised for the work'.[70]

The second draft of *Anna Livia* is a miniature version of the entire episode. It is approximately 3000 words in length, as compared with some 5500 words in the *Navire d'Argent* version (October 1925) and 8500 words in the *Wake*. Joyce enlarged this second draft early in 1924 to make his first fair copy of the chapter.

On 7 March 1924 Joyce wrote to Harriet Weaver: 'I have finished the *Anna Livia* piece'. He then went on to explain the episode.

It is a chattering dialogue across the river by two washerwomen who as night falls become a tree and a stone. The river is named Anna Liffey. Some of the words at the beginning are hybrid Danish-English. Dublin is a city founded by Vikings. The Irish name is . . . Town of Ford of Hurdles. Her Pandora's box contains the ills flesh is heir to. The stream is quite brown, rich in salmon, very devious, shallow. The splitting up towards the end (seven dams) is the city abuilding. Izzy will be later Isolde (cf. Chapelizod).[71]

The '*Anna Livia* piece' referred to in this letter is obviously the first fair copy, which was sent to Miss Weaver on 8 March 1924.[72] This fair copy was the basic narrative upon which Joyce elaborated for the next four years.

During 1925 Joyce made extensive changes in *Anna Livia* while preparing the episode for publication in a London journal, *The Calendar*.[73] Proofs for *The Calendar* had actually reached a point corresponding with page 211 of the *Wake* when the printer objected to certain passages; Joyce, who had learned from his experiences with *Dubliners* and *Ulysses* the futility of negotiation, immediately withdrew the episode. This incident is described in a prefatory note to the publication of *Anna Livia* in *Le Navire d'Argent*:

Une revue londonienne 'The Calendar' devait publier en Octobre un fragment d'une oeuvre inédite de James Joyce. —Les imprimeurs anglais, une fois de plus, refusèrent d'imprimer INTÉGRALEMENT *le texte. La Rédaction du 'Calendar' pria l'auteur de faire des modifications. M.*

Joyce refusa de discuter la question et retira son manuscrit. — Nous pensons être agréables à ceux de nos lecteurs qui aiment la littérature anglaise en leur offrant dans ce numéro le texte incriminé.[74]

Evidently the partial galley proof printed for *The Calendar* was used in setting up the first parts of the episode for *Navire d'Argent*. The galley sheets bear a number of marginal corrections and additions.[75]

After the publication of *Anna Livia* in *Navire d'Argent* (October 1925) the galley sheets for *transition* No. 8 provide the next evidence of revision. They are dated by the printer '7 Octobre 1927'. One day later, on October 8th, Joyce wrote to Miss Weaver that he was working very hard on a 'final' revision of *Anna Livia* upon which he was prepared to stake everything.[76] It was during this recasting of the episode for *transition* No. 8 that the inclusion of river-names became the dominant mode of alteration.

Joyce did not finish correcting the *transition* proofs until the end of October 1927. On the 28th of that month he wrote to Miss Weaver:

I did not really finish with Δ till 6 yesterday evening. The final proofreading alone took me five hours. I do not know what to think of it. Hundreds of river names are woven into the text. I think it moves.[77]

However, the elaboration of the episode did not end with the appearance of *transition* No. 8. 'I have not yet done with Mrs A. L.', Joyce wrote on October 29th.

t. [*transition*] 8 is out I believe but I am still working away on the final revise, as I am to read it to a group of 'critics' on Wednesday next. The stream is now rising to flood point but I find she can carry almost anything. ... When I have at last got her off into the Irish sea I shall sigh with relief.[78]

Since he was using this episode as a test of his new techniques

Joyce must have approached the reading with trepidation; but it was a success.

The reading seems to have made a profound impression on the audience (about 25 people of the world's 1500 million) but I have been literally doubled in two from fatigue and cramp ever since—in which plight I am also now. I was much better this morning but began to work again this afternoon. . . .

t. 8 has not yet arrived. I read from an advance copy.[79]

Later in this same week of frantic work there were additional changes: 'Since it [*transition* No. 8] came out I have woven into the printed text another 152 rivernames and it is now final as it will appear in the book'.[80] But, as usual, the appearance of finality was an illusion. *Anna Livia* underwent several more stages of intensive revision before it was published in book form by the firm of Crosby Gaige in October 1928.[81]

The Crosby Gaige *Anna Livia*, a handsome limited edition with a Preface by Padraic Colum, was the culmination of five years of exhausting labour. At last Joyce had achieved the final revision upon which he would stake everything.[82] He considered the Crosby Gaige text the justification of *Work in Progress*, a vindication of his experiments and a triumph for his method. It is substantially the same as *Finnegans Wake* I. viii. Joyce's revisions of *Anna Livia* after 1928 were negligible, and for all practical purposes we may consider that the making of the episode terminated with the Crosby Gaige text. As we have observed before, Joyce had fully developed his complex 'final' method by 1928; during the next ten years he rounded out the *Wake*'s structure and recast the entire work in the style he had already attained in pieces such as *Anna Livia Plurabelle*.

The opening passage of *Anna Livia* remained virtually unchanged throughout Joyce's revisions, as did the marvellous last paragraph where the coming of night and the metamorphosis of the washerwomen into stone and tree are completely embodied in the movement of the words. The close of the first fair copy, written early in 1924, is almost identical with the ending of the episode in *Finnegans Wake*.

Can't hear with the waters of. The chittering waters of. Flittering bats, fieldmice bawk talk. Ho! Are you not gone ahome? What Tom Malone? Can't hear with bawk of bats, all the liffeying waters of. Ho, talk save us! My foos woon't moos. I feel as old as yonder elm. A tale told of Shaun or Shem? All Livia's daughtersons. Dark hawks hear us! Night! Night! My ho head halls. I feel as heavy as yonder stone. Tell me of John or Shaun? Who were Shem and Shaun the living sons or daughters of? Night now! Tell me, tell me, tell me, elm! Nighty night! Tell me tale of stem or stone. Beside the rivering waters of, hitherand-thithering waters of. Night![83]

The changes in the passage after early 1924 were minor: 'Nighty night!' was altered to 'Night night!' in the first type-script,[84] 'foos woon't moos' to 'foos won't moos' in the second typescript.[85] 'Tell me tale' becomes 'Telmetale' in the Faber & Faber edition of *Anna Livia*, while 'Tom Malone' and 'the liffeying' were changed to 'Thom Malone' and 'thim liffeying' in the last-minute revisions before publication of the *Wake*.

No better measure of the development of *Anna Livia* can be found than the increase in river assocations. Joyce kept adding more and more river-names until over 500 were included in the 1928 Crosby Gaige text.[86] The evolution of the following passage from the *Wake*, which contains a number of allusions to rivers, reflects the evolution of the entire episode.

Do you tell me that now? I do in troth. Orara por Orbe and poor Las Animas! Ussa, Ulla, we're umbas all! Mezha, didn't you hear it a deluge of times, ufer and ufer, respund to spond? You deed, you deed! I need, I need! It's that irrawaddyng I've stoke in my aars. It all but husheth the lethest zswound. Oronoko! (FW 214/5–10)

The only part of this passage found in the first complete draft of the episode is the opening exchange between the two washerwomen: 'Do you tell me that now? I do, in troth'.[87] This remains the same through several versions, but on the second typescript the exclamation 'Oronoko!' is added.

Do you tell me that now? I do, in troth. Oronoko![88]

'Oronoko!', spoken by one of the washerwomen who thinks she sees the figure of the 'great Finnleader himself' (FW 214/11) in the dusk, is a complex portmanteau word. It is the name of a variety of Virginia tobacco; perhaps HCE is being compared with Sir Walter Ralegh! It is certainly a reference to Aphra Behn's novel *Oroonoko, or the Royal Slave* (1678); HCE is Oroonoko in his rôles of lover and liberator. 'Oro' as a rendering of the Greek for 'mountain' is appropriate for the recognition of HCE. But 'oro' is also a Latin verb meaning 'to speak' or 'to entreat', so 'Orono-' may mean 'please be quiet, hush!' Thus 'Oronoko!' can be paraphrased as: 'Hush! I think I see HCE, the great lover and hero, rover and liberator, looming like a mountain'. Meanwhile, Anna Livia is equated with another of the world's rivers, the Orinoco.

With the addition of 'Oronoko!' the final limits of the passage are established. The version printed in *Le Navire d'Argent* (1925) shows no further changes, but the galley proofs for *transition* (1927) reveal considerable expansion.

Do you tell me that now? I do in troth. And didn't you hear it a deluge of times? You deed, you deed! I need, I need! It's that irrawaddyng I've stuck in my aars. It all but husheth the lethest sound. Oronoko![89]

On the galley sheet the two sentences prior to 'Oronoko!' are a marginal insertion, and 'I need, I need!' is a revised form of 'I died, I died!' 'Deluge' is an obvious river allusion. 'Irrawaddyng', 'aars', and 'lethest' combine the basic meanings 'wadding', 'ears', and 'slightest' with three more rivers: the Irrawaddy, the Aar, and the Lethe.

The passage remained the same in the *transition* text. However, in the first revision of *transition* Joyce inserted 'Ussa, ulla, we're umbas all!' between 'I do in troth' and 'And didn't you hear it a deluge of times?'[90] In the second revision he made further changes and additions to produce this text:

Do you tell me that now? I do in troth. Orara poor Orbe and poor Las Animas. Ussa, Ulla, we're umbas all! Mezha, didn't you hear it a deluge of times? You deed, you deed! I need, I need! It's that irrawaddyng I've stoke in my aars. It all but husheth the lethest sound. Oronoko![91]

'And' has been altered to 'Mezha' in order to combine 'ha' with the Indian river Meza and the Italian *mezza*, suggesting that the cries of the washerwomen are *mezza voce*. 'Stuck' is now 'stoke', an allusion to the river Stokes. 'Orara poor Orbe and poor Las Animas' merges the Spanish *orar por Orbe y por Las Ánimas* ('to pray for the Earth and the Souls of the Dead') with three river names: the Orara in New South Wales, the Orba in Italy, and the Orb in France. 'Ussa' and 'Ulla' are both names of Russian rivers, as well as the near (us *ça*) and far (you *là*) banks of the river. 'Umbas' is a portmanteau combination of *umbra* (shade, ghost) and the Umba river of East Africa.

The Crosby Gaige *Anna Livia* (1928) reveals a further expansion of the passage.

Do you tell me that now? I do in troth. Orara por Orbe and poor Las Animas! Ussa, Ulla, we're umbas all! Mezha, didn't you hear it a deluge of times, ufer and ufer, respund to spond? You deed, you deed! I need, I need! It's that irrawaddyng I've stoke in my aars. It all but husheth the lethest sound. Oronoko![92]

'Ufer' is the German for 'shore' or 'river bank'; it also suggests the Ufa, a Russian river, and is the word for a medium-sized fir pole or spar. Spar after spar is spinning down the Liffey, destined for the pond in 'spond'. There are, furthermore, suggestions of the spondaic sounds made by the spars in 'respund to spond'.

This passage from the 1928 text is identical with that in the *Wake* except for one detail, the change of 'sound' to 'zswound' which occurred in 1936 while Joyce was preparing Part I of the *Wake* for final publication.[93]

Besides revealing the accumulation of river-names and allusions, the revisions of this passage indicate how Joyce's additions merge into the associational flow of the narrative. The fragment in distorted Spanish is related to a sentence some eight lines before: 'I've heard tell that same brooch of the Shannons was married into a family in Spain' (FW 213/33–34). Nightfall and the metamorphosis of the two washerwomen determine the basic movement of the passage. The strained exclamations 'You deed, you deed! I need, I need!' embody this movement: hearing is becoming more difficult, life is slipping from the women as light fails. 'Las Animas', 'umbas', 'Mezha', 'husheth', and 'lethest' all point toward the darkness of death and dreams.

A more extended illustration of the development of *Anna Livia Plurabelle* is found in the growth of the paragraph on pages 208–209 of *Finnegans Wake* beginning 'Hellsbells, I'm sorry I missed her!' Here is the first version of the paragraph (late 1923); in transcribing it I have incorporated the marginal insertions.

hellsbells, I'm sorry I missed her. Everyone who saw her said the sweet little lady seemed a bit queer. Funny poor dear she must have looked. Dickens a funnier ever you saw. There was a gang of surfacemen boomslanging & plugchewing lying & leasing, on Lazy Wall & as soon as they seen who was in it says one to the other: Between you & me & the wall beneath us as round as a hoop Alp has doped.[94]

This passage contains the essential situation elaborated upon in the succeeding revisions. The first fair copy reveals further expansion, and the paragraph appears in the original typescript as follows:

Hellsbells, I'm sorry I missed her! But in which of her mouths? Was her nose alight? Everyone that saw her said the douce little lady looked a bit queer. Funny poor frump she must have looked. Dickens a funnier ever you saw. Well for her she couldn't see herself. There was a gang of drouthdropping surfacemen, boomslanging and plug-chewing, lolling and leasing on Lazy Wall and as soon as they saw her trip by in profile and twigged who it was was in it, Lucan's fish and Dublin's poison, says one to another: Between me and you and the granite we're warming as round as a hoop Alp has doped.[95]

The revisions which were made in this passage before it reached print in *Le Navire d'Argent* (October 1925) reflect a new aim, the emphasizing of Anna Livia's riverlike nature. To fulfil this aim, 'Lucan's fish' becomes 'Avondale's fish', introducing the Avon, and ALP is described as 'Making soft mullet's eyes at her boys dobelong'.[96] Joyce made so many changes at this stage of composition that several sheets of the original second typescript, including the one containing this paragraph, had to be retyped. The following insertion is in the margin of the first version:

I warrant that's why she murrayed her mirror. She did? Mersey me![97]

Here Joyce has introduced the Mersey and the Murray, a river in South Australia: but in doing so he has almost completely obscured the original (and more important) meaning of 'muddied'. Similarly, on the first carbon he inserted the Cher by converting 'she must have turned' to 'she must have charred'; changed 'in which of her mouths' to 'in whelk of her mouths', thus incorporating a 'whelk' and the Elk river of Tennessee; and altered 'nose' to 'naze', the term for a headland or promontory.[98] In each of these cases the original meaning was greatly obscured by the additional allusion.

After additional revisions, the paragraph was published in *Le Navire d'Argent* as follows:

Hellsbells, I'm sorry I missed her! Sweet umptyum and nobody fainted. But in whelk of her mouths? Was her naze alight? Everyone that saw her said the dowse little delia looked a bit queer. Lotsy trotsy, mind the poddle. Funny poor frump she must have charred. Kickhams a rummier ever you saw. Making saft mullet's eyes at her boys dobelong. And they crowned her the queen of the may. Of the may? You don't say! Well for her she couldn't see herself. I warrant that's why she murrayed her mirror. She did? Mersey me! There was a gang of drouthdropping surfacemen, boomslanging and plugchewing, lolling and leasing on Lazy Wall by the Jook of Yoick's and as soon as they saw her meander by in her grasswinter's weeds and twigged who was under her deaconess bonnet, Avondale's fish and Clarence's poison, says one to another: *Between me and you and the granite we're warming, as round as a hoop, Alp has doped.*[99]

The introduction of river-names and associations became the dominant mode of revision after 1925. The sentence below appears for the first time on the galley proofs for *transition* (1927), following 'Lotsy trotsy, mind the poddle!'.

Missus, be good and don't fol in the say![100]

'Missus' suggests 'Mississippi', the Fol is a Turkish river, while 'say' reminds one of the Seine and is the Irish pronunciation of 'sea'. On the same proofs the 'gang of drouthdropping surfacemen' becomes 'a koros of drouthdropping surfacemen': the Körös is a river in Hungary.[101] And the 'surfacemen' are definitely identified as the Twelve Customers at Earwicker's pub by the insertion of four words ending in '-ation': 'in contemplation of the fluctuation and the undification of her filimentation'.[102] All of these changes may be seen in the *transition* text:

Hellsbells, I'm sorry I missed her! Sweet umptyum and nobody fainted. But in whelk of her mouths? Was her naze alight? Everyone that saw her said the dowse little delia looked a bit queer. Lotsy trotsy, mind the poddle! Missus, be good and don't fol in the say! Funny poor frump she must have charred. Kickhams a rummier ever you saw. Making saft mullet's eyes at her boys dobelong. And they crowned her the queen of the may. Of the may? You don't say! Well for her she couldn't see herself. I warrant that's why the darling murrayed her mirror. She did? Mersey me! There was a koros of drouthdropping surfacemen, boomslanging and plugchewing, fruiteyeing and flower-feeding, in contemplation of the fluctuation and the undification of her filimentation, lolling and leasing on Lazy Wall by the Jook of Yoick's and as soon as they saw her meander by in her grasswinter's weeds and twigged who was under her deaconess bonnet, Avondale's fish and Clarence's poison, says one to another, Wit-upon-Crutches to Master Bates: *Between me and you and the granite we're warming, as round as a hoop, Alp has doped.*[103]

The revisions which occurred between *transition* and the Crosby Gaige *Anna Livia* reinforce the river motif. On the first set of corrected pages from *transition* 'sweet umptyum' is merged with the Gumti, an Indian river, to form 'sweet gumptyum'.[104] Among the changes on the second set, 'Lazy Wall' becomes 'Lazy Waal' (the Waal is a Dutch river), and 'Funny poor frump' becomes 'Fenny poor hex', thus introducing the fens that surround a watercourse and the Hex, a river in the Cape of Good Hope.[105] On the galley proofs for the Crosby Gaige version three additions —'wharfore', 'all eelfare week', and 'that marritime way'—carry the process further by weaving 'wharf', 'eel', and 'maritime' into the narrative.[106] All these changes are found in the Crosby Gaige text:

Hellsbells, I'm sorry I missed her! Sweet gumptyum and nobody fainted. But in whelk of her mouths? Was her naze alight? Everyone that saw her said the dowce little delia looked a bit queer. Lotsy trotsy, mind the poddle! Missus, be good and don't fol in the say! Fenny poor hex she must have charred. Kickhams a frumpier ever you saw. Making saft mullet's eyes at her boys dobelong. And they crowned her their chariton queen, all the maids. Of the may? You don't say! Well for her she couldn't see herself. I recknitz wharfore the darling murrayed her mirror. She did? Mersey me! There was a koros of drouth-dropping surfacemen, boomslanging and plugchewing, fruiteyeing and flowerfeeding, in contemplation of the fluctuation and the undification of her filimentation, lolling and leasing on North Lazers' Waal all eelfare week by the Jukar Yoick's and as soon as they saw her meander by that marritime way in her grasswinter's weeds and twigged who was under her deaconess bonnet, Avondale's fish and Clarence's poison, says an to aneber, Wit-upon-Crutches to Master Bates: *Between our two southsates and the granite they're warming, or her face has been lifted or Alp has doped.*[107]

With the exception of four minor changes made in 1936–37[108] the 'Hellsbells' paragraph in the *Wake* is identical with the same passage in the Crosby Gaige text. While tracing its development we have, of necessity, neglected many of the alterations and expansions in order to concentrate upon one aspect of Joyce's method, his attempt to create a style that embodies the characteristics of all rivers. We might have approached the revisions from many other viewpoints: Joyce's interest in 'sound-patterns', in rhyme and alliteration; his desire for compression and allusiveness; his striving for 'simultaneous' presentation. But all these artistic aims are intimately connected with the accumulation of river-names.

Joyce incorporated hundreds of river-names into *Anna Livia Plurabelle* in order to make the episode 'expressive' of his heroine's riverlike nature. As Padraic Colum says in his Preface to the Crosby Gaige edition, which Joyce liked 'immensely':

> *Anna Livia Plurabelle* is concerned with the flowing of a River [the Liffey] . . . And the River itself, less in magnitude than the tributary of a tributary of one of the important rivers, becomes enlarged until it includes hundreds of the world's rivers. How many rivers have their names woven into the tale of *Anna Livia Plurabelle?* More than five hundred, I believe.[109]

Colum compares a passage from *Portrait of the Artist* in which Stephen muses by the Liffey with the opening lines of *Anna Livia*, and then comments: 'The first passage gives us the sight of the River, the second gives us the River as it is seen and heard and felt'.[110] Here are the two passages:

In the distance along the course of the slow-flowing Liffey slender masts flecked the sky, and, more distant still, the dim fabric of the city lay prone in haze. Like a scene on some vague arras, old as man's weariness, the image of the seventh city of Christendom was visible to him across the timeless air, no older nor more weary nor less patient of subjection than in the days of the thingmote.

O

tell me all about Anna Livia! I want to hear all about Anna Livia. Well, you know Anna Livia? Yes, of course, we all know Anna Livia. Tell me all. Tell me now.[111]

Colum's comparison is just. The first passage is an evocative description of the river and city which acts as a background to Stephen's *ennui*. The second is an onomatopoeic *rendering* of the river. But Colum does not tell us how the inclusion of partially-distorted river-names intensifies the impression made by the episode's flowing rhythms. The discovery of these names in the text is a conscious act of the mind, like the solving of a puzzle, and their impact is quite different from the immediate impact of sound-patterns. Edmund Wilson raises this problem in *Axel's Castle*:

Joyce has improved it [*Anna Livia*] in making the texture denser, but this enrichment also obscures the main outlines and somewhat over-solidifies and impedes the dim ambiguous fluidity of the dream— especially when it takes the form of introducing in the final version puns on the names of some five hundred rivers. And as soon as we are aware of Joyce himself systematically embroidering on his text, deliberately inventing puzzles, the illusion of the dream is lost.[112]

In *The Wound and the Bow* Wilson makes the same protest, and voices his doubt that the introduction of several hundred rivers has 'really made Anna Livia any more riverlike'.[113] He feels that Joyce should have halted his recasting of the episode somewhere between the *transition* and Crosby Gaige versions.[114] It is significant that Wilson's critical judgment led him to choose as a terminal point the precise stage in Joyce's revisions when—as this chapter demonstrates—the inclusion of river-names became almost an obsession. No one can deny that many of the original and important aspects of *Anna Livia* are buried under river-names and allusions added in the last stages of revision; and it is a damning commentary on Joyce's method that a study of earlier versions often provides important clues to the meaning of a passage in the final text. *Anna Livia Plurabelle*, the culmination of Joyce's efforts to anastomose matter and form, displays the extreme virtues and defects of the 'expressive' method.

It may seem paradoxical, after these strictures on Joyce's techniques, to re-assert the claim that *Anna Livia Plurabelle* is an artistic success. Yet it is a success, and precisely because Joyce retained throughout his complex revisions the sound of the human voice, the gossipy tones of the two washerwomen who are our link with the episode's 'realistic' setting. When *Anna Livia* is read aloud the river-allusions rarely obscure this dialogue, although to the visual imagination they may appear to do so. The following sentence from *Navire d'Argent*,

Who was the first that ever burst?[115]

had become by 1928

Waiwhou was the first thurever burst?[116]

To the eye it may seem that Joyce clouded the original 'narrative' meaning by inserting the Waihou and Thur rivers; but to the ear the sense is still clear.

One wishes that Joyce had halted his revision of *Anna Livia* sooner, before his emphasis on 'expressive' form became disproportionate to the effects that he actually achieved. But a process of elaboration has no inherent boundaries. Given techniques which permit expansion through a distortion of word and syntax, the process of revision is invariably a movement away from the original 'narrative' situation, a movement which shifts the artist's emphasis from primary to secondary qualities of language. There is no inherent limit to the amount of elaboration which can occur, and beyond a certain point the process of revision ceases to enrich the basic text and begins to obscure it. The method leads to inclusiveness rather than that 'discrimination and selection'—the phrase is Henry James's—which produces the greatest art. Furthermore, in his attempts to fuse matter and form, and to exploit the musical potentialities of language, Joyce often neglected the rational structure of his language. The defects of *Anna Livia* demonstrate the radical limitations of any work of art, perfection in one mode of expression necessitating the sacrifice of other modes.

NOTES FOR SECTION III

1. Prior to final publication *Finnegans Wake* was known only by the provisional title *Work in Progress*. For a table of composition which includes the published fragments, see Appendix C. This table should serve as an adjunct to the present chapter.

2. The *Finnegans Wake* MSS. were presented to the British Museum in 1951 by Harriet Shaw Weaver. For a detailed description of this material, see Appendix A.

3. Bruno is mentioned in 'The Day of the Rabblement' (1901), and Joyce discussed Bruno's philosophy with his Italian teacher at University College (see *The Critical Writings of James Joyce*, ed. Ellsworth Mason and Richard Ellmann, New York, 1959, p. 132). In 1903 Joyce reviewed J. Lewis McIntyre's *Giordano Bruno* for the Dublin *Daily Express* (*Critical Writings*, 132–34). His passionate interest in Vico's philosophy began during the Trieste years (Gorman, 332).

4. For Joyce's use in *Finnegans Wake* of legends and anecdotes familiar to his family, see Ellmann, 558; Gorman, 274; *Letters*, 396.

5. There is also a hint in *Ulysses* of the story 'How Buckley Shot the Russian General'. The assassination of the Russian governor-general of Finland, General Bobrikoff, by a Finnish patriot is mentioned in the *Aeolus* episode (133). The event actually happened on Bloomsday (16 June 1904).

6. In the Lockwood Memorial Library, University of Buffalo, there is a voluminous notebook dating from that transitional period which spans Joyce's late work on *Ulysses* and his preliminary efforts on the *Wake* (approx. 1920–25). In this notebook Joyce reviewed his earlier works and the episodes of *Ulysses*, apparently as a prelude to his first labours on the *Wake*; the notebook reveals the economy of Joyce's artistic methods, since it contains numerous entries salvaged from the composition of earlier works. The compilation of this elaborate collection of notes and summaries testifies to the reflexive nature of Joyce's art, and to the close connection between *Finnegans Wake* and those works which preceded it. For a brief description of the notebook, see *James Joyce: sa vie, son oeuvre, son rayonnement*, ed. Bernard Gheerbrant, Paris, La Hune, 1949, item 346.

7. *Letters*, p. 202. For further details concerning the genesis of *Finnegans Wake*, see my article in *Notes and Queries*, CXCVIII (October 1953), 445–47. For a discussion of the early fragments, with copious quotations, see M. J. C. Hodgart, 'The Earliest Sections of *Finnegans Wake*', *James Joyce Review*, I (February 1957), 3–18.

8. *Letters*, p. 202. The early versions of these fragments are bound in at the end of British Museum Add. Ms. 47485. The fair copy and first drafts of 'Tristan and Isolde' were given to Harriet Weaver by Joyce in August 1923, after she had typed the fragment for him. In July 1938 he requested a new copy of the typescript, having apparently misplaced the original (Slocum, p. 146, item a. ix).

9. Frank Budgen, 'Joyce's Chapters of Going Forth by Day', in *James Joyce: Two Decades of Criticism*, ed. Seon Givens, New York, 1948, p. 347. See also *Letters*, 406.

10. These drafts (Add. Ms. 47488, ff. 99–101) are bound in at the end of Add. Ms. 47485.

11. Add. Ms. 47488, f. 99.

12. *Ibid.*, f. 101.

13. *Letters*, 205.

14. *Letters*, 213. JJ to HSW, 24 March 1924.

15. The development of 'Tristan and Isolde' and 'Mamalujo' may be traced in B. M. Add. Ms. 47481.

16. *Letters*, 204. JJ to HSW, 9 Oct. 1923.

17. *Ibid.*

18. *Letters*, 205. JJ to HSW, 17 Oct. 1923.

19. Frank Budgen, 'James Joyce', in *James Joyce: Two Decades of Criticism*, p. 24.

20. *Letters*, 205. JJ to HSW, 17 Oct. 1923.

21. B. M. Add. Ms. 47471-B.

22. *Letters*, 210, 212.

23. Letter to Harriet Weaver, 15 March 1924. Miss Weaver kindly provided me with extracts from Joyce's letters concerning *Work in Progress*, and although previous arrangements made by the Joyce Estate prevent me from quoting some of these extracts I have used them to determine many dates and facts in this chapter.

24. *Letters*, 222. JJ to HSW, 9 Nov. 1924.

25. *Letters*, 222. JJ to HSW, 16 Nov. 1924.

26. Unpublished letter to Harriet Weaver, 11 April 1925.

27. *Letters*, 227.

28. *Letters*, 234.

29. *Letters*, 241. The symbols used in this letter belong to a series Joyce began to employ in his notes and letters as early as 1923. Several of them appear in the red-backed notebook (B. M. Add. Ms. 47471-B) dating from late 1923. The major symbols are grouped together in a footnote on page 299 of the *Wake*: 'The Doodles family, ⌐, Δ, ⊣, X, □, Λ, Ⳇ'. The significance of the more important of these signs was given by Joyce in a letter to Harriet Weaver of 24 March 1924 (*Letters*, 213). Here are the symbols for the Earwicker family:

⌐—in any position this is HCE, the hero.

Δ—ALP, his wife.

⊣—Issy, the daughter.

Λ—Shaun.
              the twins.
Ⳇ—Shem.

The signs have important graphic meanings, recapitulating the principal qualities and functions of the personalities they represent. Commenting on ⊔ as employed in the first chapter of the *Wake*, Joyce said that 'the sign in this form means H C E interred in the landscape' (*Letters*, 254). Similarly, ⊒ signifies HCE's resurrection, ⌐ his presence in prehistoric form (Stonehenge), and E his existence as Earwicker, the Everyman of modern times. Thus ⊒, ⌐, E, and ⊔ represent the four-part Viconian cycle (Resurrection, Heroic accomplishment, Civil extension, and the Fall) which is the major structural principle of the *Wake*.

In contrast, Anna Livia's symbol (**Δ**) is the same in every position, just as she herself remains constant during the cyclic changes of her husband. The 'delta' reminds the reader of her character as all rivers; it is also a sexual emblem. It was probably at Joyce's request that a red equilateral triangle was placed on the cover of the *Anna Livia Plurabelle* pamphlet published by Faber and Faber in 1930.

The meanings of the children's signs are equally important. ⊣ is a toppled T, and may represent the daughter in her rôle of Isolde, for whom T-ristram falls. Ɛ reminds one of Shem's impotence in life: it is his father's symbol without the penis. Shaun's sign (Λ) is his mother's without its base: although it is Shaun's function to carry and deliver ALP's letter, he is lacking in a basic understanding of his mother's secret.

30. *Letters*, 241. JJ to HSW, 7 June 1926.

31. See Slocum, p. 146, item E. 7. a. vii. The notebook is now B. M. Add. Ms. 47482-A.

32. *Letters*, 242. JJ to HSW, 15 July 1926.

33. Add. Ms. 47482-A; the draft of chapter 1 begins on f. 83.

34. *Letters*, 246. JJ to HSW, 8 Nov. 1926.

35. See *Letters*, 247–48.

36. Add. Ms. 47482-A, f. 83.

37. *transition* No. 1 (April 1927), 9.

38. Joseph Campbell and H. M. Robinson, *A Skeleton Key to 'Finnegans Wake'*, London, 1947, p. 33.

39. *Ibid.*

40. *Stephen Hero*, ed. Theodore Spencer, New Edn., New York, 1955, p. 97.

41. See *Letters*, 249.

42. Unpublished letter to Harriet Weaver, 26 July 1927.

43. 'My Friend James Joyce', in *James Joyce: Two Decades of Criticism*, p. 7.

44. See the following chapter for a detailed analysis of *Anna Livia's* evolution.

45. *Letters*, 273–74. In this dictated letter to Harriet Weaver (23 Oct. 1928) Joyce provides an extensive gloss for the passage.

46. *transition* Nos. 6, 11, 12.

47. The early version comes from *transition* No. 15 (February 1929), p. 233; the revised version is found in *Haveth Childers Everywhere*, Paris and New York, 1930, pp. 18–20. This passage is now found on pp. 535–36 of the *Wake*.

48. *Letters*, 290.

49. Unpublished letter to Harriet Weaver, 22 Sept. 1930.

50. *Letters*, 295.

51. See *Letters*, 326–28.

52. See Eugene Jolas, 'My Friend James Joyce', in *James Joyce: Two Decades of Criticism*, p. 11; and Louis Gillet, *Claybook for James Joyce*, trans. Georges Markow-Totevy, New York, 1958, pp. 90–91.

I

53. *transition* No. 22 (February 1933), 59. Reprinted without change in the *Wake* (232/24–26).

54. Page 59.

55. FW 257/3–28 and *transition*, pp. 75–76.

56. Joseph Campbell and H. M. Robinson, *A Skeleton Key to 'Finnegans Wake'*, pp. 90–91.

57. From the Prefatory Letter to Charles Duff's *James Joyce and the Plain Reader*, London, 1932, pp. 12–13.

58. Harry Levin, *James Joyce*, London, 1944, pp. 125–26.

59. See in this connection Slocum, 146–47, items E. 7. a. ix and a. xiii.

60. Gorman, 224.

61. B. M. Add. Ms. 47475 contains the version of Part I from which the first galleys of *Finnegans Wake* were set up. It is composed of *transition* texts for episodes i–vii, and the Criterion Miscellany (Faber and Faber) text for *Anna Livia*; all are corrected and augmented. The following is inscribed in the front of the volume, in Joyce's hand: 'MS Part I completed 11 July 1936 Paris J J'.

62. Add. Ms. 47476-A, f. 1.

63. Louis Gillet, *Claybook for James Joyce*, trans. Georges Markow-Totevy, p. 94.

64. See Gorman, 347.

65. The section of *Finnegans Wake* published separately under the title *Anna Livia Plurabelle* covers pp. 196–216. Most of the notes, drafts, typescripts and galley sheets which record the growth of the episode were given to Harriet Weaver, and are now in the British Museum. Other material is in the Slocum Collection of the Yale University Library: see (12) and (13) below. The following is a chronological outline of the distinct stages in the episode's development:

(1) The Earliest Draft, British Museum Add. Ms. 47471-B, ff. 74–78.

(2) The Second Draft, Add. Ms. 47471-B, ff. 79–90.

(3) The First Fair Copy, Add. Ms. 47474, ff. 106–123.

(4) The First Typescript, Add. Ms. 47474, ff. 124–140.

(5) The Second Typescript, three sets, Add. Ms. 47474, ff. 141–202.

(6) Galley Proofs for *The Calendar*, Add. Ms. 47474, ff. 203–206.

(7) 'From Work in Progress', *Le Navire d'Argent*, I (October 1925), 59–74.

(8) Galley Proofs for *transition* No. 8 (November 1927), Add. Ms. 47474, ff. 208–225.

(9) *transition* No. 8 (November 1927), 17–35.

(10) Corrected Pages of *transition* No. 8, first set, Add. Ms. 47474, ff. 226–246.

(11) Corrected Pages of *transition* No. 8, second set, Add. Ms. 47474, ff. 247–257.

(12) The copy of *transition* No. 8 used to set up the Crosby Gaige edition of *Anna Livia*. Now in the Slocum Collection at the Yale University Library.

(13) Galley Proofs for the Crosby Gaige *Anna Livia*. Add. Ms. 47474, ff. 258–271, and three sets in the Slocum Collection.

(14) *Anna Livia Plurabelle*, New York, Crosby Gaige, October 1928.

(15) *Anna Livia Plurabelle*, London, Faber & Faber, June 1930.

(16) Corrected copies of (15), used to set up the galleys of *Finnegans Wake* I. viii. Add. Ms. 47475, ff. 75–90 & 164–179.

(17) Three sets of galley proofs for *Finnegans Wake* I. viii. Add. Ms. 47476-A, ff. 118–132 & 261–275, and Add. Ms. 47476-B, ff. 411–425.

(18) *Finnegans Wake* (1939), pp. 196–216.

For a more detailed discussion of the process of revision, see my article on 'The Evolution of Joyce's *Anna Livia Plurabelle*', *Philological Quarterly*, XXXVI (January 1957), 36–48.

Those who wish to examine the evolution of *Anna Livia Plurabelle* for themselves should consult *Anna Livia Plurabelle: The Making of a Chapter*, ed. Fred H. Higginson, Minneapolis, 1960. Professor Higginson has reduced the complex development of *Anna Livia* to six basic texts, but an ingenious system of notes and symbols enables the reader to reconstruct every important stage in the growth of the episode. This edition also contains a brief but useful Introduction in which Professor Higginson discusses Joyce's linguistic aims and explicates a sample passage.

66. The recording of this passage (FW 213–16) is available in several pressings. See Slocum, 173.

67. Slocum, 145, item E. 7. a. i.

68. Add. Ms. 47471-B, f. 74.

69. *Ibid.*, f. 77.

70. Leon Edel, 'James Joyce and His New Work', *University of Toronto Quarterly*, IX (October 1939), 76. The section of Edel's article covering pp. 75–79 is a brief but excellent analysis of the evolution of *Anna Livia*, based on examination of the published versions. Two other critics have considered the development of *Anna Livia*: Edmund Wilson, *Axel's Castle*, New York, 1950, pp. 235, 301–03 (first published in 1931); and Theodore B. Dolmatch, 'Notes and Queries Concerning the Revisions in *Finnegans Wake*', *Modern Language Quarterly*, XVI (June 1955), 142–48.

71. *Letters*, 212–213.

72. The envelope is bound in at the beginning of the fair copy in Add. Ms. 47474.

73. See note 65, stages 4–6.

74. *Le Navire d'Argent*, I (October 1925), 59.

75. Add. Ms. 47474, ff. 203–206.

76. Information from an unpublished letter to Harriet Weaver, 8 Oct. 1927.

77. *Letters*, 259.

78. *Letters*, 260.

79. *Letters*, 260. JJ to HSW, 4 Nov. 1927.

80. *Letters*, 261. JJ to HSW, 9 Nov. 1927.

81. See note 65, stages 10–13.

82. See note 76.

83. Add. Ms. 47474, f. 118.

84. *Ibid.*, f. 138.

85. *Ibid.*, f. 159.

86. Padraic Colum, Preface to the Crosby Gaige *Anna Livia*, p. xi.

87. Add. Ms. 47471-B, ff. 88–89.

88. Add. Ms. 47474, ff. 157 and 165.

89. *Ibid.*, f. 224.

90. *Ibid.*, f. 244.

91. *Ibid.*, f. 256.

92. Crosby Gaige *Anna Livia*, p. 55.

93. Add. Ms. 47475, reverse of ff. 89 and 178.

94. Add. Ms. 47471-B, f. 87 and reverse of f. 86. In this case, as in most, I have not attempted to record all of Joyce's false starts and rejected phrases, but have aimed at transcribing the text as it stands after his deletions and marginal insertions.

95. Add. Ms. 47474, ff. 133–134.

96. *Ibid.*, ff. 162 and 153.

97. *Ibid.*, f. 162.

98. *Ibid.*, f. 178.

99. *Le Navire d'Argent*, p. 69.

100. Add. Ms. 47474, f. 218.

101. *Ibid.*

102. *Ibid.*

103. *transition* No. 8, pp. 28–29.

104. Add. Ms. 47474, f. 238.

105. *Ibid.*, reverse of f. 253.

106. *Ibid.*, f. 266.

107. Crosby Gaige *Anna Livia*, pp. 38–40.

108. On the reverse of f. 85 of Add. Ms. 47475, 'saft mullet's' is changed to 'mush mullet's', 'dobelong' to 'dobelon', and 'says an to aneber' to 'sedges an to aneber'; on f. 127 of Add. Ms. 47476-A 'deaconess bonnet' is altered to 'archdeaconess bonnet'.

109. Preface to Crosby Gaige *Anna Livia*, pp. vii, xi. Joyce's approval of the Preface is recorded in *Our Friend James Joyce*, by Mary and Padraic Colum, New York, 1958, p. 139.

110. Preface, p. ix.

111. Preface, pp. viii–ix.

112. *Axel's Castle*, p. 235.

113. *The Wound and the Bow*, Revised Edn., London, 1952, p. 235.

114. *Ibid.*

115. *Le Navire d'Argent*, p. 65.

116. Crosby Gaige *Anna Livia*, p. 19.

IV

THE WHOLE JOURNEY

No writer ever revised more carefully or used his rough notes and sketches more economically than Joyce. Each of his works grows out of its predecessor and prepares the way for a succeeding work already visualized in tentative form. There is a sense in which we can say that James Joyce wrote only one book, a continuous effort to endow his own life and the Dublin of his youth with universal significance. T. S. Eliot was one of the first to recognize this continuity, and in his foreword to the catalogue of the 1949 Joyce exhibition in Paris he made a plea for criticism based on a total assessment of Joyce's achievement:

> Joyce's writings form a whole; we can neither reject the early work as stages, of no intrinsic interest, of his progress towards the latter, nor reject the later work as the outcome of decline. As with Shakespeare, his later work must be understood through the earlier, and the first through the last; it is the whole journey, not any one stage of it, that assures him his place among the great.[1]

Eliot's insistence on the unity of Joyce's art has been supported by our examination of the manner in which *Ulysses* and *Finnegans Wake* developed. Earlier chapters have shown that the methods Joyce employed in the last stages of his 'journey'—the techniques which shaped *Ulysses* and the *Wake*—evolved from the formal aims of his previous fiction. It remains to take some measure of the relationship between these final methods and the visions of reality found in his last two works.

For a variety of personal and environmental reasons Joyce ceased during his later years to assimilate significant new experiences into his artistic imagination.[2] With all their complexity and freshness of technique, *Ulysses* and *Finnegans Wake* are but new visions of the world described in *Dubliners*, *Stephen Hero* and *A Portrait*. We can find evidence of Joyce's tenacious hold on the concrete elements of his early experience on every page of his notebooks and rough drafts. No incident capable of symbolic extension was ever wasted. An extreme instance of this economy is provided by the history of a single passage, a short description of the Joyce kitchen which failed to make its way into *Stephen Hero* and *Portrait* but was finally included in *Ulysses*. Here is the passage as it appears in a discarded fragment of Joyce's autobiographical novel:

The rank smell of fried herrings filled the kitchen and the bare table was strewn with greasy plates to which glutinous fish-bones and crusts were stuck by a congealing white sauce. Clammy knives and forks were abandoned here and there. A big soot-coated kettle, which had been drained of the last dregs of shell cocoa, sat in the midst of the disorder beside a large jam-jar still half-full of the oatmeal water which had served for milk. Under the table the tortoiseshell cat was chewing ravenously at a mess of charred fishheads and eggshells heaped on a square of brown paper.[3]

Although there was no place for this 'epiphany' in the final version of *Portrait*, Joyce refused to relinquish it. At first he set down a brief version of the scene on a note-sheet for the *Cyclops* chapter, but later he transferred the abbreviated reminder to another note-sheet containing material for the *Eumaeus* episode. Ultimately an expanded version of the passage was incorporated into *Eumaeus*.

Joyce never wasted material drawn from his early observation, but as this material was hoarded and re-worked without the benefit of fresh perspectives it was gradually distorted, becoming by the time it reached *Finnegans Wake* the substance of myth or burlesque. As the gap between Joyce's creative life and his early experience widened and the emotions of his youth receded into the past, he desperately placed more and more emphasis on a literal fidelity to details of place and personality. This insistence on accuracy went far beyond the ordinary requirements of verisimilitude and bordered on the obsessive, as when he went to great trouble to ascertain whether a man of Bloom's agility could actually climb over the area railings of No. 7 Eccles Street and drop to the ground unhurt.[4] This exaggerated need for literal fidelity must be seen as a part of Joyce's desperate attempt to give his developing techniques the authority of actual experience.

Joyce's constant re-working of the same basic situations could only be successful and fresh if he constantly altered his techniques, new techniques rather than new experience being the source of vitality. What we are confronted with in Joyce's total work is repeated treatment of the same body of experience by a variety of modern techniques, ranging from those of Flaubert and Chekhov to those of Mallarmé's *Coup de Dés*.[5] Viewed as a single achievement, his writing recapitulates three generations of literary experiment. This is one of the reasons why Joyce has not been a seminal force in modern literature, but rather the terminator of traditions.

Joyce lived through an age in which the traditional forms of mind and society had become problematical, perhaps even illusory. As a stay against this chaos he fell back on the arbitrary forms created by language, and it is no wonder that as we trace his art from *Dubliners* through *Finnegans Wake* words cease to be signs or symbols of external reality and become dynamic units which create a new vision of reality. It is customary to compare Joyce's elaborate correspondences with those of Dante, but the comparison is specious. The extrinsic order of the *Divine Comedy* reflects a view of man's destiny which informs Dante's entire work, whereas Joyce's mechanical frames are too often neutral patterns, arbitrary scaffolds. This is but to say that in Joyce we find many of the medieval impulses freed from the experiences which gave them life: techniques tend to exist for their own sake, *imposing* order rather than reflecting it.

We have seen that one may view Joyce's artistic development as an all-consuming movement toward simultaneity of effects. As his work on *Ulysses* progressed he sought to attach more and more significance to the instant of time, until finally the balance was tipped and the symbolic significance of events overshadowed the events themselves. The symbolic meanings ceased to be logical extensions of the moment and became patterns imposed from without. When in the first story of *Dubliners* the paralysis of the old priest is taken as an emblem of Ireland's spiritual paralysis, we feel that Joyce's theory of the 'epiphany' has proved its worth and that he has discovered a completely adequate natural symbol. But when the slamming of a door in *Finnegans Wake* is transformed into the Viconian thunderclap that ends civilization as well as the children's games, Joyce is operating from a different premise. The conception of a natural or rational connection between event and significance has been abandoned, and the burden of association thrown entirely on language. Although *Finnegans Wake* is saturated with realistic details drawn from Joyce's memory and his knowledge of Irish history and myth, we feel that these details have been separated from the reality of his early experience and are counters in a vast linguistic experiment.

Finnegans Wake was the result of Joyce's restless desire to explore the full possibilities of the techniques he developed while working on *Portrait* and *Ulysses*; it shows the extreme virtues and limitations of his art. At one and the same time the *Wake* is too abstract and too concrete. Paradoxically, it displays a detailed point-by-point fidelity to Joyce's early experiences without reflecting—as do *Portrait* and *Ulysses*—a full sense of the reality of those experiences. The result is an infinitely rich texture combined with a tedium of basic thought. That sense of 'felt life' which Henry James considered the essence of literary form infuses Joyce's artifice by fits and starts.

Perhaps I can explain this failure I find in the *Wake* by reference to the work of another great Irishman, W. B. Yeats. One of the wonders of Yeats's late work (*The Tower* and after) is the contrast between the direct vision of his poetry and the involved, often confused concepts of *A Vision*. Most readers are thankful that Yeats embodied the eccentricities and complex abstractions of his thought in *A Vision*, leaving his poetry as a vehicle for concrete expression. Yet Joyce, when Eugene Jolas read *A Vision* to him, could only regret that 'Yeats did not put all this into a creative work'.[6] Few would share Joyce's regret. All of *A Vision* that could be communicated in poetry found its way into Yeats's verse; the vast remainder that was necessary for the ordering of his mind, that cleared the way for poetic expression but did not enter into it, was relegated to the prose tract, which now serves as an adjunct to the poetry. In separating *A Vision* from his later poetry Yeats performed an act of discrimination alien to Joyce's final techniques.

It is possible to compare the complex surface pattern of the *Wake* with the 'scaffold' of correspondences Joyce erected for *Ulysses*. Both were provisional substitutes for religious faith, mechanical replacements for the orders of home, fatherland and church which Joyce had discarded. But a vital distinction must be made between the form of *Ulysses* and that of the *Wake*, even though both works were shaped by similar artistic impulses. In *Ulysses* one needs to understand the symbolic dimensions, but Joyce's techniques do not stand between the reader and the primary level of the novel, the actions of Bloom and Stephen. The words and syntax are those of conventional language, even in those final episodes which adumbrate certain techniques of the *Wake*. The action of the book is immediately accessible, and this provides the reader with an incentive for the careful study necessary to comprehend Joyce's full intent. But in *Finnegans Wake* the correspondences and accidental associations have penetrated word and syntax; they lie on the surface, in puns and neologisms, and present an initial barrier to understanding. As a result of Joyce's extended and painstaking composition by accretion the more remote and exotic connections invariably lie on the surface, and are the first to be encountered; the book may be thought of as containing many strata of allusions which are revealed to the reader in inverse order of importance. The naturalistic plot, such as it is, provides no strong incentive to exploration and discovery, and Joyce has relied almost entirely upon the 'musical' qualities of his language to establish initial communication. Only a few readers find this 'musical' quality sufficient inducement. Others, with a belief in Joyce's art based on earlier works, are willing to explore the *Wake* on faith, and for them the labour is amply rewarding. Perhaps, as more aids to explication are produced, the *Wake* will—like the once 'unreadable' *Ulysses*—become widely understood. But this would seem unlikely, since in writing *Finnegans Wake* Joyce pushed his methods to the limits of his talent and beyond. It is difficult to imagine successors to the *Wake* in the sense that *The Waste Land* and Pound's *Cantos* are successors to *Ulysses*. Joyce's failing eyesight, his vast linguistic talent, and the growing egoism of his later years produced in the *Wake* a special form; the knowledge and reading skills which it demands are in great measure peculiar to it. Perhaps this is the final pyrrhic triumph of Joyce's lifelong search for a form in which expression and substance are uniquely joined.

But whatever our caveats may be when confronted by Joyce's final work, it would be a mistake to think that Joyce was oblivious to them. Before the *Wake* was well underway he had debated, in the colloquy between Bishop Berkeley and the archdruid, the limitations and strengths of his projected work, and throughout his seventeen years of labour on the *Wake* this sense of the work's precarious nature never left him. Eugene Jolas has recalled that during the 1930's Joyce 'became more and more absorbed by meditations on the imaginative creation'. He read Coleridge and was interested in the distinction Coleridge makes between Imagination and Fancy, wondering 'if he himself had imagination'.[7]

It is easy to understand why Joyce was fascinated and disturbed by that passage near the end of Chapter XIII of *Biographia Literaria* where Coleridge distinguishes between Fancy and Imagination.

> The secondary Imagination . . . dissolves, diffuses, dissipates, in order to recreate; or where this process is rendered impossible, yet still at all events it struggles to idealize and to unify. It is essentially *vital*, even as all objects (*as* objects) are essentially fixed and dead.
>
> FANCY, on the contrary, has no other counters to play with, but fixities and definites. The Fancy is indeed no other than a mode of Memory emancipated from the order of time and space; while it is blended with, and modified by that empirical phenomenon of the will, which we express by the word CHOICE. But equally with the ordinary memory the Fancy must receive all its materials ready made from the law of association.[8]

According to Coleridge, Fancy is the 'DRAPERY' of 'poetic genius' while Imagination is the unifying power which 'forms all into one graceful and intelligent whole'.[9] If we apply these terms to *Finnegans Wake*, it is obvious that the fundamental vision displays Imagination in the Coleridgean sense; but it is also true that the 'DRAPERY' of Fancy found in the work's texture often obscures this Imaginative core. Joyce's continuous elaborations of *Work in Progress*, his multiplying of analogies, proceeded by a method which was a 'mode of Memory emancipated from the order of time and space'. I do not wish to press this distinction between Fancy and Imagination, nor its application to the *Wake*, too far; it is enough to indicate why Joyce wondered if 'he himself had imagination'. No one knew better than James Joyce the defects of his final work.

NOTES FOR SECTION IV

1. *James Joyce: sa vie, son oeuvre, son rayonnement*, ed. Bernard Gheerbrant, Paris, La Hune, 1949.
2. The biographical evidence for this assertion is too complex to be marshalled at this point in my argument; for confirmation see the later chapters of Ellmann's biography. One might claim that Joyce's reading

during the making of *Finnegans Wake* provided fresh and significant material for his imagination, but it seems more plausible to hold that this reading was controlled and directed by patterns already firmly fixed in his mind.

3. See Appendix B for a detailed history of this passage.

4. See *Letters*, 175.

5. For a study of the affinities between Joyce's work and that of Mallarmé, see David Hayman, *Joyce et Mallarmé*, 2 vols., Paris, 1956.

6. Eugene Jolas, 'My Friend James Joyce', in *James Joyce: Two Decades of Criticism*, ed. Seon Givens, New York, 1948, p. 15.

7. *Ibid.*, p. 14.

8. *Biographia Literaria*, ed. J. Shawcross, 2 vols., Oxford, 1907, I, 202.

9. *Ibid.*, II, 13.

APPENDIX A

Manuscripts Consulted

1. *Ulysses*

(a) *Notes*. In 1938 Paul Léon, who was acting as Joyce's secretary, sent a number of note-sheets for the last seven episodes of *Ulysses* to Harriet Shaw Weaver. These have since been deposited in the British Museum. On the envelope containing the sheets Joyce wrote: 'Some sheets of notes for certain episodes in *Ulysses*'. There are twenty-nine separate sheets: eighteen of these are double (folded) and eleven are single. Joyce usually wrote on both sides of a sheet; allowing for the few blank pages, there are approximately ninety sides of notes. The double sheets are approximately 12×8 inches in size when folded; the single sheets vary widely, some being $9 \times 7\frac{1}{2}$ inch sheets of graph paper. The handwriting is extremely difficult, and some of the entries are completely illegible.

The following is a census of the note-sheets by episodes:

	Double Sheets	Single Sheets	Total
Cyclops	3	0	3
Nausicaa	2	0	2
Oxen of the Sun	6	0	6
Circe	2	5	7
Eumaeus	1	2	3
Ithaca	2	4	6
Penelope	2	0	2
	18	11	29

Similar notes for a number of episodes are contained in a notebook (La Hune 252) now in the Lockwood Memorial Library, University of Buffalo (Slocum, p. 140, item E. 5. b. i).

(b) *Early Drafts of Episodes*. A number of manuscript drafts of parts of *Ulysses* were exhibited at the Librairie La Hune, Paris, in 1949; these were later acquired by the Lockwood Memorial Library, University of Buffalo. A brief description of these MSS. will be found in the La Hune catalogue, *James Joyce: sa vie, son oeuvre, son rayonnement*,

Paris, 1949, items 253, 255–259. See also the Slocum and Cahoon *Bibliography*, pp. 140–41, item E. 5. b. Slocum and Cahoon erroneously list a fragment of *Scylla and Charybdis* as being in the Buffalo collection; actually this item (La Hune 254) was lost in transit between Paris and Buffalo.

The rich collection of Joyce material recently acquired by the Cornell University Library contains an early draft of part of *Nausicaa*.

(c) *Autograph Manuscript*. Originally the property of John Quinn, this MS. was acquired by the late A. S. W. Rosenbach in 1924 and is now owned by the Philip and A. S. W. Rosenbach Foundation, Philadelphia. The episodes to *Oxen of the Sun* are substantially the same as those which appeared in the *Little Review*, and bear few revisions. Written between late 1917 and mid-1920, they do not contain the later additions made by Joyce in 1921. The episodes after *Oxen* are in intermediate form, displaying copious alterations and additions in Joyce's hand. Of the later episodes, *Eumaeus* seems nearest to completion. The draft of *Penelope* ends at p. 761 of the Random House edition.

2. *Finnegans Wake*

The notes, drafts, typescripts, and galley proofs for *Finnegans Wake* were given to Miss Weaver by Joyce over a period of years, in gratitude for her unparalleled generosity. In July of 1951 she presented the entire body of MSS. (defective only in Part II) to the British Museum. Mr. Julian Brown, who supervised the cataloguing and binding of the MSS., has grouped them wherever possible by episodes. In several cases Joyce's own notebooks have been rebound and preserved in their original form; the loose sheets have been bound into uniform volumes.

The following outline of the contents of the twenty-three volumes in the British Museum should illustrate the arrangement of the MSS. Wherever possible I have given references to the abbreviated description of the MSS. on pages 145–47 of the Slocum and Cahoon *Bibliography* (section E. 7. a.), which is based upon Miss Weaver's own catalogue.

British Museum Additional Manuscript Number	*Contents*
Add. Ms. 47471-A	An orange-coloured notebook containing the second draft of FW I. i. The first draft of I. i is in a large notebook (Add. Ms. 47482-A) with material for III. iv and 'The Triangle' (the earliest version of FW 282-304). See Slocum, item a. ii.

Add. Ms. 47471-B	The earliest draft of Part I with the exception of chapters i and vi. See Slocum, item a. i.
Add. Ms. 47472	Development of Part I, i–iv.
Add. Ms. 47473	Development of Part I, iv–vi.
Add. Ms. 47474	Development of Part I, vii–viii.
Add. Ms. 47475	The text of Part I from which the galleys of the *Wake* were set up: it is composed of the revised *transition* text for chapters i–vii, and the Faber and Faber *Anna Livia* for viii. Bears the dateline '11 July 1936 Paris' in Joyce's hand.
Add. Ms. 47476-A & B	Sets of galley proofs for Part I.
Add. Ms. 47477	Development of II. i. See Slocum, item a. vi.
Add. Ms. 47478	Material for II. ii. See also Add. Ms. 47482-A below.
Add Ms. 47479 and	Development of II. iii.
Add. Ms. 47480	
Add. Ms. 47481	Development of II. iv. See Slocum, item a. ix.
Add. Ms. 47482-A	Notebook containing material for III. iv; 'The Triangle' (earliest version of FW 282–304); and first draft of I. i. See Slocum, items a. ii, a. vii, and a. xii.
Add. Ms. 47482-B	Notebook for Shaun a–c, FW III. i–iii. See Slocum. item a. x.
Add. Ms. 47483	Development of Shaun a & b, III. i–ii.
Add. Ms. 47484-A & B	Development of Shaun c, III. iii.
Add. Ms. 47485	Folio volume of Shaun d, III. iv. Bound in at the end are the 'King Roderick O'Conor', 'Tristan and Isolde', 'St. Kevin', and 'pidgin fella Berkeley' fragments dating from 1923. See Slocum, items a. viii and a. xiii.
Add. Ms. 47486-A & B	Corrections and additions to the *transition* text of Part III.
Add. Ms. 47487	Galley proofs for Part III.
Add. Ms. 47488	Development of Part IV. See Slocum, item a. xiii.

The Slocum Collection of the Yale University Library contains the *Anna Livia* pages of *transition* No. 8 corrected by Joyce, and proofs for the Crosby Gaige *Anna Livia*. These were consulted in the preparation of Chapter III. 3. The Lockwood Memorial Library, University of Buffalo, owns the small notebooks for *Finnegans Wake* exhibited at the Librairie La Hune, Paris, in 1949 (item 157 in the La Hune catalogue); see Slocum, p. 147, item E. 7. b.

APPENDIX B

Early Vestiges of *Ulysses*

THE unity of Joyce's accomplishment is nowhere more evident than in the evolution of the texts of his major works. Phrases, characters, and long passages are deleted from one manuscript only to appear later in a different context. Thus many of the early *Epiphanies*, written in Paris during the winter and spring of 1902–03, eventually found their place in the texts of *Stephen Hero*, the *Portrait* and *Ulysses*.[1] Joyce's economical methods of revision are clearly illustrated by five manuscript sheets which were given to Harriet Weaver by Sylvia Beach in March of 1939. These sheets, fair copies in Joyce's hand of passages intended for his autobiographical novel, are evidence of the complex relationship that links *Stephen Hero* and the *Portrait* with *Ulysses*. Most important of all, they reveal his techniques of composition at the time when he began *Ulysses* and are the earliest extant fragments of that novel.

Each sheet is $8\frac{5}{16}$ by $6\frac{11}{16}$ inches (21 by 17 cms.) in size. The left-hand edges are slightly ragged, suggesting that Joyce may have cut the pages from a notebook or from larger sheets; the wide left-hand margins (2 inches) were probably intended for corrections. The five pages comprise three distinct narrative units, which I have distinguished as Fragments A, B, and C. The left-hand column below is an exact transcript of the three fragments, arranged so that textual duplications and similarities in other works and MSS. are displayed in the parallel right-hand column.[2] Deletions in Joyce's MS. are indicated by square brackets.

FRAGMENT A (three sheets)

But the echo of his laughter had been the remembrance of Doherty, standing on the steps of his house the night before, saying:

—And on Sunday I consume the particle. Christine, *semel in die*. The mockery of it all! But it's for the sake of the poor aunt. God, we must be

'Dr. Doherty and the Holy City' is one of Joyce's early (1904) notes for his autobiographical novel.[3]

'—For this, O dearly beloved, is the genuine Christine...' Spoken by Buck Mulligan (U 5).

'—The mockery of it...' Mulligan

132

human first. Doherty meets his afflicted aunt. I am writing a mystery-play in half an act. Scene: Heaven. Enter two bouzes from Leitrim wearing blue spectacles. From Leitrim! "What was it at all? Was it electric light or the *aurora borealis*?" "That was himself" "Glory be to God! It is the grandest thing I ever saw." I think that's a lovely touch. The mockery of it! Ireland secretes priests: that's my new phrase. I must go. A woman waits for me. God, the humanity of Whitman! I contain all. I embrace all. Farewell. Did you notice Yeats's new touch with the hand up. It's the Roman salute. *Salve!* Pip, pip! O, a lovely mummer! Dedalus, we must retire to the tower, you and I. Our lives are precious. I'll try to touch the aunt. We are the super-artists. *Dedalus and Doherty have left Ireland for the Omphalos—*

(U 5, 8). Buck Mulligan's aunt (U 6, 7, 8).

Mulligan: '—I have conceived a play for the mummers, . . . (*a national immorality in three orgasms*)' (U 214). Compare Bloom's question in the *Circe* episode: '*Aurora borealis* or a steel foundry?' (U 427).

'—The mockery of it . . .' Mulligan (U 5, 8).

Compare the allusion to Whitman on p. 18 of *Ulysses*: 'Do I contradict myself? Very well then, I contradict myself'. Doherty-Mulligan and Whitman are linked in both contexts.

'Couldn't you do the Yeats touch?' (U 213).

'—But a lovely mummer, he [Mulligan] murmured to himself. Kinch, the loveliest mummer of them all' (U 7).

'We must go to Athens. Will you come if I can get the aunt to fork out twenty quid?' (U 6).

This is the Martello tower, setting for the first episode of *Ulysses*. Buck Mulligan calls it 'the *omphalos*' (U 19). On p. 9 of *Ulysses* Stephen thinks: 'To ourselves . . . new paganism . . . omphalos.'

The rank smell of fried herrings filled the kitchen and the bare table was strewn with greasy plates [on] to which [lay] glutinous fish-bones and crusts were stuck by a congealing white sauce. Clammy knives and forks were abandoned here and there. A big soot-coated kettle, [sat in] which had been drained of the last dregs of shell cocoa, sat in the midst

This description of the Dedalus kitchen appears twice in abbreviated form among the note-sheets for *Ulysses*. First, with notes for the *Cyclops* episode: 'Dilly's Kitchen: oatmeal water, cat devours charred fishheads and eggshells heaped on square of brown paper, shell cocoa in kettle, sootcoated'. And again among notes for the *Eumaeus* of the disorder beside a large jam-jar still half-full of the oatmeal water which had served for milk. Under the table the tortoiseshell cat was chewing ravenously at a mess of charred fish [guts] heads and egg-shells heaped on a square of brown paper.

episode: 'Dilly's Kitchen: oatmeal water, cat devours charred fishheads & eggshells heaped on brown paper, shell cocoa in sootcoated kettle'.

The scene finally reached print in *Ulysses* as follows: '... Stephen's mind's eye being too busily engaged in repicturing his family hearth the last time he saw it, with his sister, Dilly, sitting by the ingle, her hair hanging down, waiting for some weak Trinidad shell cocoa that was in the sootcoated kettle to be done so that she and he could drink it with the oatmeal water for milk after the Friday herrings they had eaten at two a penny, with an egg apiece for Maggy, Boody and Katey, the cat meanwhile under the mangle devouring a mess of eggshells and charred fish heads and bones on a square of brown paper in accordance with the third precept of the church to fast and abstain on the days commanded, it being quarter tense or, if not, ember days or something like that' (U 604).

His mother, flushed and red-eyed sat by the range. Stephen, weary of the strife [lean] of tongues, leaned against the japanned wall of the fire-place. Noises and cries and laughter echoed in the narrow yard: and from time to time a nose was flattened against the window pane, fingers tapped mockingly and a young voice, faint and high in the dim evening, asked if the genius had finished his phrenology.

—It is all over those books you read. I knew you would lose your faith. I'll burn every one of them—

'Mrs Daedalus began to cry. Stephen, having eaten and drunk all within his province, rose and went towards the door:

—It's all the fault of those books and the company you keep. Out at all hours of the night instead of in your home, the proper place for you. I'll burn every one of them. I won't have them in the house to corrupt anyone else.

Stephen halted at the door and turned towards his mother who had now broken out into tears:

—If you had not lost [the] your faith—said Stephen—you would burn me along with the books—

—If you were a genuine Roman Catholic, mother, you would burn me as well as the books.'[4]

FRAGMENT B (one sheet)

shed his blood for all men they have no need of other aspersion.

Doherty's gibes flashed to and fro through the torpor of his mind and he thought without mirth of his friend's face, equine and pallid, and of his pallid hair, grained and hued like oak. He had tried to receive coldly these memories of his friend's boisterous humour, feeling that his coarseness of speech was not a blasphemy of the spirit but a coward's mask, but in the end the troop of swinish images broke down his reserve and went trampling through his memory, followed by his laughter:

I'm the queerest young fellow
   that ever you heard.
My mother's a jew, my father's
   a bird.
With Joseph the joiner I cannot
   agree
So here's to disciples and Calvary!

My methods are new and are
   causing surprise.
To make the blind see I throw
   dust in their eyes. . . .

'If I told them there is no water in the font to symbolise that when Christ has washed us in blood we have no need of other aspersions.'[5]

On page 5 of *Ulysses* Mulligan's face is described as 'equine in its length'. He has 'light untonsured hair, grained and hued like pale oak'. See also page 40 of *Ulysses*: 'The oval equine faces, Temple, Buck Mulligan, Foxy Campbell'.

Buck Mulligan chants this stanza of the Ballad of Joking Jesus, with two others, to Stephen in the first episode of *Ulysses* (U 20–21).

'EDWARD VII
(*Levitates over heaps of slain in the garb and with the halo of Joking Jesus, a white jujube in his phosphorescent face.*)

My methods are new and are
   causing surprise.
To make the blind see I throw
   dust in their eyes' (U 576).

FRAGMENT C (one sheet)

rage:
—Devil out of hell! We won! We crushed him to death! Fiend!—

The door slammed behind her.

Mr Casey, freeing his arms from his holders, suddenly bowed his head on his hands with a sob of pain.
—Poor Parnell!—he cried loudly—My dead King!—

He sobbed loudly and bitterly.

Stephen, raising his terror-stricken face, saw that his father's eyes were full of tears.

With the exception of minor differences in punctuation, this passage is the same as the conclusion of the dinner-table scene in *A Portrait of the Artist as a Young Man*.

These three fragments are obviously from a late draft of Joyce's autobiographical novel. Internal evidence alone would be sufficient to establish this fact. The finished style, the condensation of the scene between Stephen and his mother, and the form 'Dedalus' (instead of the earlier 'Daedalus' of *Stephen Hero*) point to a date of composition considerably after the completion of the *Stephen Hero* manuscript in 1906.[6] The five sheets are similar in size, quality of paper, and handwriting, and probably date from the same period. Fragment C is practically identical with its counterpart in the final version of the *Portrait*, and this fact, together with the *Ulysses* adumbrations, suggests a late dating of the fragments. The terminal date is obviously 1915, since the *Portrait* appeared serially in the *Egoist* between February 1914 and September 1915. The earlier limit is established by Joyce's own account (written in 1920) of the burning of the *Stephen Hero* manuscript, which I see no reason to doubt even though it conflicts with the account given in Herbert Gorman's biography:

The 'original' original I tore up and threw into the stove about eight years ago in a fit of rage on account of the trouble over *Dubliners*. The charred remains of the MS were rescued by a family fire brigade and tied up in an old sheet where they remained for some months. I then sorted them out and pieced them together as best I could and the present MS is the result.[7]

Whatever one's final decision may be as to the burning of *Stephen Hero*, this letter suggests that Joyce dated the final phase of his work on the *Portrait* from 1911–12. Richard Ellmann's research has indicated that

Joyce drafted the first three chapters of *Portrait* in 1907–08, but may have delayed the completion of chapters four and five until as late as 1914–15.[8]

The deletions in Fragment A, particularly of 'sat in' and 'lean', are such as would occur in a hasty copying from another manuscript; they appear to be the result of the eye out-distancing the hand, and suggest that at least one other version of the scene may lie between *Stephen Hero* and this text. These copying errors support a date for the fragments well along in the final period of composition. However, the materials of Fragments A and B may date from as early as 1904–05. Joyce knew the 'Ballad of Joking Jesus' in 1905, and associated it with Oliver St. John Gogarty (Buck Mulligan); furthermore, in the original plan of his autobiographical novel, conceived in 1904–05, the Martello tower episode was intended to be the cause for Stephen's leaving Ireland.[9]

For the critic of *Ulysses*, Fragments A and B are of immense importance. Doherty is a prototype of Buck Mulligan, an intermediary between the Oliver St. John Gogarty of real life and the fictionalized Gogarty of *Ulysses*. His mocking attitude is the same as that of Mulligan, his features are described in the same words: 'equine and pallid, . . . pallid hair, grained and hued like oak'. There is also a suggestion of Cranly's condescension in his manner. In the opening chapter of *Ulysses* Mulligan links his arm in Stephen's, and Stephen thinks: 'Cranly's arm. His arm' (U 9). 'Cranly' and 'Buck Mulligan' are both listed as characters for the *Telemachus* episode on one of the *Ulysses* note-sheets, an indication of the importance Joyce attached to Stephen's association of the two companions. Doherty is Mulligan as he was to have appeared in the *Portrait*, before Joyce decided to make these incidents the centre of the first episode in *Ulysses*.

Fragments A and B both begin with the memory of Doherty-Mulligan's mocking laughter tormenting Stephen's mind. A probable context for Fragment B is established by the broken sentence which opens it, an echo from *Stephen Hero*. In the early novel Stephen attends a Good Friday service and watches two old women cross themselves with dry hands when leaving, not knowing why the font is empty. At the end of this scene Joyce pencilled: 'If I told them there is no water in the font to symbolise that when Christ has washed us in blood we have no need of other aspersions'. Joyce may have intended Stephen's recollection of Doherty's blasphemous gibes to come at the end of this scene. There is no trace of the incident in the final version of *A Portrait*.

Doherty's recitation of the Ballad of Joking Jesus is resented by Stephen in the manuscript for the same reason it is resented in *Ulysses*: Stephen cannot regain his faith because of the inconsistencies humorously emphasized in the Ballad, but he is revolted by Mulligan's light treatment of the blasphemy. Disbelief is as serious a matter to Stephen as belief. The first stanza of the Ballad is chanted by Mulligan in the *Telemachus* episode, along with two others, but the verses which close the fragment ('My methods are new and are causing surprise. / To make the blind see I throw dust in their eyes') do not appear until *Circe*, where they are spoken by the apparition of Edward VII. Thus the 'usurping' Mulligan and the 'usurping' British government are placed in the same category; both are enemies of Ireland and of honest belief or disbelief, and Joyce the exiled Irish-Catholic judges them together.

Fragment A provides an insight into Joyce's method of composition. The paragraph referring to Doherty contains many 'seeds' for the first episode of *Ulysses*. The Martello tower is already an ironic symbol of retreat. As 'the *Omphalos*' it is an emblem of the human navel, the source of life, and of the stone in the temple of Apollo at Delphi that was supposed to mark the centre of the earth. It represents a mystical centre which can provide no refuge for Stephen; he is forced to give the key to Mulligan, and the tower has become the home of Haines (Fr. *haine*, 'hate') and the Black Mass. One is reminded of Stephen's bitter reverie in the *Proteus* episode:

Will you be as gods? Gaze in your omphalos.
Hello. Kinch here. Put me on to Edenville.
(U 39)

Doherty's contempt for the Mass is consistent with Buck Mulligan's parody of the sacrament in *Ulysses*. '*Semel in die*' prepares the way for Mulligan's daily mockery of the Mass while shaving, and in both contexts the ritual is treated as a magician's trick. Similarly, every element in the first paragraph of Fragment A is related to the *Telemachus* episode in some way. For instance, the reference to Whitman in the fragment differs from that in *Ulysses*, but the essential fact, the similarity between the blustering animalism of Doherty-Mulligan and that of Whitman, remains unchanged.

The paragraph in Fragment A describing the kitchen of Joyce's home had a fascinating career of revisions. It is reminiscent of many naturalistic descriptions of the sordid conditions of Stephen's home in

Stephen Hero, and in the context it emphasizes the dreary background of Mrs. Dedalus' faith. The paragraph was not included in the *Portrait*, but it obviously epiphanized for Joyce the hopeless wretchedness of his home, since it persists in outline form through two of the note-sheets for *Ulysses* and appears in an expanded version in the *Eumaeus* episode. During this development the context of the descriptive passage was altered: in *Eumaeus* it is Stephen's vivid memory of his home as he last saw it, some time after his mother's death, and in this connection it represents the spiritual and physical poverty of his family which Stephen fears will 'drown' him.[10]

The evolution of this passage illustrates two important characteristics of Joyce's revisions. First, it demonstrates that his portrayals of his own life and home in the *Portrait* and *Ulysses* are faithful in spirit but not always historically accurate. Often scenes were shifted from one context to another, and substantially altered, during the course of revision. The rewritings of *Stephen Hero*, the *Portrait*, and *Ulysses* mirror Joyce's shifting attitude towards his early life: the movement is from the personal to the impersonal, from individual to general significance, from autobiography to biography. Joyce freely altered facts in his struggle towards a 'dramatic' ideal.

Secondly, the changes in the passage illustrate the way in which a word or phrase is used by Joyce in his notes to suggest whole scenes or large segments of dialogue. The sequence of concrete images found on the *Ulysses* note-sheet ('oatmeal water, cat devours charred fishheads & eggshells heaped on brown paper, shell cocoa in sootcoated kettle') was used by Joyce to recall to his mind the entire scene. It is interesting to note that the images here are *visual*: later, in the notes for *Ulysses* and *Finnegans Wake*, rhythm and sound play an important part in effecting the recall. Having the broad outline of his work already in mind, Joyce used these abbreviated notations to remind himself of the material available for each stage of the composition. The method reflects the static nature of his art.

Stephen's argument with his mother, a matter of one paragraph in Fragment A, covered five pages in *Stephen Hero*. In the *Portrait* it is simply alluded to in a conversation between Stephen and Cranly:

—Cranly, I had an unpleasant quarrel this evening.—
—With your people?—Cranly asked.
—With my mother.—
—About religion?—
—Yes—Stephen answered.[11]

In Fragment A all the descriptive details of the *Stephen Hero* account have been eliminated; the result is an increase of emotional intensity in the portrayal of his mother's grief and in Stephen's embittered reply. Diffuse personal arguments have been retired in favour of a single intense passage. But even this concentrated presentation seemed too personal, too much a figure of his own revolt, to be retained by Joyce in the *Portrait*.

Fragments A and B reveal the characteristics of Joyce's technique at the time when he began *Ulysses*. The compression demanded by his theory of 'epiphany' and the aloof tone resulting from his notion of 'stasis' are everywhere evident. Already apparent are the allusiveness and symbolic 'thickening' (as in the '*Omphalos*' figure) that give his later works a dense texture comparable to that of poetry. The flow of Doherty's words through Stephen's mind has the quality of the 'interior monologue' in *Ulysses*, and the treatment of time found in *Ulysses* and *Finnegans Wake* can be discovered in these fragments. Both of the scenes involving Doherty come to Stephen as memories prompted by his present situation, thus illustrating Joyce's desire to use memory as an agent for investing every moment with the richness of layer upon layer of associated experiences.

NOTES FOR APPENDIX B

1. See James Joyce, *Epiphanies*, ed. O. A. Silverman, Lockwood Memorial Library, University of Buffalo, 1956.

2. I am indebted to Mr. J. Mitchell Morse, who pointed out several parallels that I had not noticed. See his note in PMLA, LXXI (December 1956), 1173.

3. Gorman, 136.

4. *Stephen Hero*, ed. Theodore Spencer, New Edn., New York, 1955, p. 135.

5. *Stephen Hero*, p. 121. Added in pencil at the end of Chapter XX of the MS.

6. For the dating of *Stephen Hero*, see Theodore Spencer's comments in his Introduction (*Stephen Hero*, pp. 7–9), and Joyce's letter to Grant Richards dated 13 March 1906 (Gorman, 148).

7. *Letters*, 136; Joyce to Harriet Weaver, 1 Jan. 1920. Herbert Gorman says that in 1908 Joyce 'burned a portion of *Stephen Hero* in a fit of momentary despair and then started the novel anew in a more compressed form' (Gorman, 196). Gorman may have mistaken the date, or he may, as Stanislaus Joyce suggests, have confused an attempt to burn *Dubliners* with the burning of *Stephen Hero*. We shall probably never know the exact details of this important event. The various accounts are summarized on pp. 136–137 of the Slocum and Cahoon *Bibliography* (item E. 3. d.).

8. Ellmann, 274, 279, 365.
9. See Ellmann, 212–215.
10. See *Ulysses*, p. 240.
11. *A Portrait of the Artist*, New York, The Modern Library, 1928, p. 281.

APPENDIX C

A Chronology of Joyce's Work in Progress, 1914–1939

THIS chronology of Joyce's writing and publication from 1914 to 1939 is partially a summary of facts already presented, and partially a repository for information which lay outside my argument. It is based on the works of Ellmann and Gorman, the *Letters*, the Slocum and Cahoon *Bibliography*, and many other biographical and bibliographical sources. Contemporary accounts have been given priority over memoirs and reminiscences, and I have used my own judgment in resolving contradictory opinions. Joyce's method of collecting material, his habit of working on more than one episode at the same time, and his incessant revisions make it virtually impossible to set precise time-limits for the writing of each episode. However, one can establish the order in which the episodes were written, and distinguish the major stages of composition.

Writing

1914

In March Joyce began work on *Ulysses* by 'setting down . . . preliminary sketches for the final sections'.

In the spring Joyce suspended work on *Ulysses* and resumed work on the notes for *Exiles*. In August he began drafting the play, which occupied much of his time during 1914–15.

Publication

A Portrait of the Artist appeared serially in the *Egoist* from Vol. I, No. 3 (2 Feb. 1914) to Vol. II, No. 9 (1 Sept. 1915).

The first edition of *Dubliners* was published in London by Grant Richards Ltd. on June 15th.

1915

By mid-1915, when Joyce left Trieste for Zürich, he had reached the third episode (*Proteus*).

Exiles finished in September.

1916

Part of 'Hamlet' chapter (*Scylla and Charybdis*) already drafted.

1917

During October-December, while convalescing in Locarno, Joyce prepared *Telemachus*, *Nestor*, and *Proteus* for publication.

1918

By October Joyce had drafted the first eight episodes and was working on the ninth (*Scylla and Charybdis*).

Telemachus: Little Review, IV, March, pp. 3–22.

Nestor: Little Review, IV, April, pp. 32–45.

Proteus: Little Review, V, May, pp. 31–45.

Calypso: Little Review, V, June, pp. 39–52.

Lotus-eaters: Little Review, V, July, pp. 37–49.

Hades: Little Review, V, September, pp. 15–37.

Aeolus: Little Review, V, October, pp. 26–51.

1919

By mid-1919 Joyce had drafted episodes 10 and 11 (*Wandering Rocks & Sirens*) and was at work on 12 (*Cyclops*).

Cyclops was finished in September, and before Joyce returned to Trieste (October) he began to plan the next episode (*Nausicaa*).

Lestrygonians (1): *Little Review*, V, January, pp. 27–50.

Lestrygonians (2): *Little Review*, V, February–March, pp. 58–62.

Scylla and Charybdis (1): *Little Review*, V, April, pp. 30–43.

Scylla and Charybdis (2): *Little Review*, VI, May, pp. 17–35.

Wandering Rocks (1): *Little Review*, VI, June, pp. 34–45.

Wandering Rocks (2): *Little Review*, VI, July, pp. 28–47.

Sirens (1): *Little Review*, VI, August, pp. 41–64.

Sirens (2): *Little Review*, VI, September, pp. 46–55.

Cyclops (1): *Little Review*, VI, November, pp. 38–54.
Cyclops (2): *Little Review*, VI, December, pp. 50–60.

. . . . .

Nestor: Egoist, VI, January–February, pp. 11–14.
Proteus: Egoist, VI, March–April, pp. 26–30.
Hades (1): *Egoist*, VI, July, pp. 42–46.
Hades (2): *Egoist*, VI, September, pp. 56–60.
Wandering Rocks (partial): *Egoist*, VI, December, pp. 74–78.

1920

Nausicaa, begun in Zürich in the autumn of 1919, was finished in Trieste early in 1920.

In February Joyce began work on the next episode, *Oxen of the Sun*, which he had been planning for some time.

Oxen completed in May.

Joyce began intensive work on *Circe* as soon as he arrived in Paris (9 July). While writing *Circe* he found relief in reworking the first episode of the *Nostos* (*Eumaeus*) which already existed in some form.

Circe was finished near the end of the year.

Cyclops (3): *Little Review*, VI, January, pp. 53–61.
Cyclops (4): *Little Review*, VI, March, pp. 54–60.
Nausicaa (1): *Little Review*, VI, April, pp. 43–50.
Nausicaa (2): *Little Review*, VII, May–June, pp. 61–72.
Nausicaa (3): *Little Review*, VII, July–August, pp. 42–58.
Oxen of the Sun (partial): *Little Review*, VII, September–December, pp. 81–92.

1921

By February *Eumaeus* was finished and *Ithaca* underway.

Work on *Ithaca* continued through October, although *Penelope* was being written at the same time.

144

Penelope was actually completed before *Ithaca* so that Valery Larbaud might read the book's close while preparing his lecture on *Ulysses* (given December 7th).

Completion of *Ithaca* on October 29th terminated the composition of *Ulysses*, although Joyce continued to revise on the proofs.

It must be remembered that much of Joyce's time during 1920–21 was spent in recasting the earlier episodes and revising the later ones. Proof-reading began in June 1921 and continued throughout the year.

1922

The first edition of *Ulysses* was published in Paris by Shakespeare & Co. on February 2nd.

1923

March: Joyce wrote his first piece since the conclusion of *Ulysses*, the King Roderick O'Conor fragment (now FW 380–82). See *Letters*, p. 202.

July–August: Joyce drafted the Tristan and Isolde fragment (later included in FW II. iv); the St. Kevin episode (FW 604–06); and 'pidgin fella Berkeley' (FW 611–612).

September: By the middle of this month Joyce had 'finished' a draft of 'Mamalujo' (FW II. iv).

The notebook containing rough drafts of all the episodes in Part I except i and vi (British Museum Add. Ms. 47471-B) must have been filled before the end of 1923.

1924

January–March: Joyce was working on I. v, I. vii, and I. viii.

In March Joyce began the 'Shaun the Post' section (FW Part III).

During the remainder of 1924 Joyce continued to revise the episodes in Part I already written, and to compose the 'four watches' of Shaun (FW III. i–iv).

'From Work in Progress', *Transatlantic Review*, I, April, pp. 215–23 (FW II. iv).

1925

The composition of Shaun's 'four watches' continued through 1925, interrupted from time to time by the need for revising episodes from Part I before their initial publication.

In early April Joyce was correcting copy for the *Criterion*, and late in the month he was faced with the proofs for the *Contact Collection*.

By the end of August Joyce had begun the last 'watch' of Shaun (FW III. iv), and on November 5th he reported that he had 'almost made a first draft of Shaun d' (FW III. iv).

'From Work in Progress', *Contact Collection of Contemporary Writers*, Paris [May], pp. 133–36 (now FW 30–34).
'Fragment of an Unpublished Work', *Criterion*, III, July, pp. 498–510 (FW I. v).
'From Work in Progress', *Navire d'Argent*, I, October, pp. 59–74 (FW I. viii).
'Extract from Work in Progress', *This Quarter*, I, Autumn–Winter, 1925–26, pp. 108–23 (FW I. vii).

1926

In April Shaun abcd (FW Part III) was put aside as 'finished', after several months of intensive revision.

In the summer Joyce wrote 'a piece of the studies' called 'The Triangle', later 'The Muddest Thick That Was Ever Heard Dump'. This eventually became the middle section of II. ii.

In the autumn Joyce drafted the opening episode, FW I. i.

1927

In 1927 Joyce was revising Part I for publication in *transition*.

In the summer he composed I. vi as a connective episode between 'The Hen' (I. v) and 'Shem the Penman' (I. vii).

'Opening Pages of a Work in Progress', *transition*, No. 1, April, pp. 9–30 (FW I. i).

'Continuation of a Work in Progress', *transition*, No. 2, May, pp. 94–107 (FW I. ii).

transition, No. 3, June, pp. 32–50 (FW I. iii).

transition, No. 4, July, pp. 46–65 (FW I. iv).

transition, No. 5, August, pp. 15–31 (FW I. v).

transition, No. 6, September, pp. 87–106f. (FW I. vi).

transition, No. 7, October, pp. 34–56 (FW I. vii).

transition, No. 8, November, pp. 17–35 (FW I. viii).

1928

In the early months Joyce revised Shaun abc for publication in *transition*.

In the spring he reworked *Anna Livia Plurabelle* (FW I. viii) for publication in book form.

Trouble with his eyes prevented Joyce from writing during most of the latter half of 1928.

transition, No. 11, February, pp. 7–18 (FW 282–304).

transition, No. 12, March, pp. 7–27 (FW III. i).

transition, No. 13, Summer, pp. 5–32 (FW III. ii).

Anna Livia Plurabelle, New York, Crosby Gaige, October (FW I. viii).

1929

Joyce began to revise his 'fables' ('The Mookse and the Gripes', 'The Muddest Thick That Was Ever Heard Dump', 'The Ondt and the Gracehoper') in late 1928 and continued the process through the spring of 1929.

transition, No. 15, February, pp. 195–238 (FW III. iii).

Tales Told of Shem and Shaun, Paris, The Black Sun Press, August (FW 152–59, 282–304, 414–19).

transition, No. 18, November, pp. 211–36 (FW III. iv).

1930

Joyce began working on II. i in September.

Haveth Childers Everywhere, Paris and New York, June (FW 532–54).
Anna Livia Plurabelle, London, Faber and Faber, June (FW I. viii).

1931

Personal difficulties kept Joyce virtually idle in 1931.

Haveth Childers Everywhere, London, Faber and Faber, May (FW 532–54).

1932

Finnegans Wake II. i was completed in 1932, in spite of great personal difficulties.

Two Tales of Shem and Shaun, London, Faber and Faber, December (FW 152–59 and 414–19).

1933

During the period 1933–37 most of Joyce's effort was devoted to the composition of FW II, ii and iii.

transition, No. 22, February, pp. 49–76 (FW 219–59).

1934

The Mime of Mick Nick and the Maggies, The Hague, The Servire Press, June (FW 219–59).

1935

transition, No. 23, July, pp. 109–29 (FW 260–75 and 304–08).

1936

In July Joyce noted that Part I was 'completed'. It was submitted to Faber and Faber for printing.

1937

The galley sheets for Part I began to appear in the spring: the sheet for page one bears the printer's date '12 March 1937'.

transition, No. 26, February, pp. 35–52 (FW 309–31).
Storiella As She Is Syung, London, Corvinus Press, October (FW 260–75 and 304–08).

1938

While the galleys for the other sections were being corrected, Joyce was completing Parts II and IV. It was not until mid-November that the process of composition came to an end; the *Wake*'s final passage was the last to be written. Corrections and alterations were made on proof through January 1939, some of them by telegram.

transition, No. 27, April–May, pp. 59–78 (FW 338–55).

1939

Joyce received the first bound copy of *Finnegans Wake* in time for his birthday, February 2nd.

Finnegans Wake, London, Faber and Faber; New York, The Viking Press, May 4th.

INDEX

151